HOLLYWOOD LOVE STORIES

ROBYN KARNEY

HOLLYWOOD LOVE STORIES

ROBYN KARNEY

OCTOPUS BOOKS

ACKNOWLEDGMENTS

The author wishes to record her gratitude to the numerous skilled and diligent biographers whose efforts eased her path and gave her much reading pleasure. Where sources are directly used they are credited in the relevant passages. The author would also like to express her appreciation to her colleague Ronald Bergan and her editor Carolyn Bailey for their unfailing help and support.

The publishers thank the following for providing the photographs in this book: Camera Press 108; Ronald Grant Archive 134, 178; Kobal Collection 91, 127, 152; Photo Source 32, 57; Rex Features 78; Syndication International 6, 46, 164. Cover Photography: Kobal collection above and centre; Rex Features/L Dale Gordon below

Editor: Carolyn Bailey
Designer: Brazzle Atkins
Production Controller: Shane Lask

First Published 1987
by Octopus Books Ltd
59 Grosvenor Street
London W1
© 1987 Octopus Books Limited
ISBN 0 7064 2984 2
Printed in Great Britain

CONTENTS

RICHARD BURTON
— AND —
ELIZABETH TAYLOR

'There comes a time during the making of a movie when the actors become the characters they play…. That happened today,' Walter Wanger, the producer of *Cleopatra*, noted in his diary on 22 January 1962. 'The cameras turned and the current was literally turned on. It was quiet and you could almost feel the electricity between Elizabeth Taylor and Burton.' It wasn't long before Wanger discovered that his stars were not merely acting. Yet their first meeting ten years previously, at the Hollywood home of Stewart Granger and Jean Simmons, had produced hardly any sparks at all. 'I first met Elizabeth when she was nineteen. I thought she was the most beautiful and sullen creature I had ever met – difficult, unreachable, unmanageable, unobtainable, impenetrable, and *difficult*.' She thought him too egocentric and, apart from throwing a few four-letter words in his direction, coolly ignored him, much to his chagrin. Afterwards, in reply to friends' questions about the screen's loveliest teenager, Burton described her as 'Dark. Dark. She's dark. She probably shaves.' Love at first sight it wasn't!

A decade later, they co-starred in the most expensive film ever made. On the first day they met on the set of *Cleopatra* at the Cinecitta Studios in Rome, Elizabeth, knowing Burton's reputation as a womanizer, wondered what his opening gambit would be. All he could muster was, 'Has anybody ever told you that you're a very pretty girl?' Returning to her dressing-room, she informed her assistants that Cleopatra had received a tribute from Wales and it wasn't very much. It was out of such inauspicious beginnings that Hollywood's greatest and most publicized love story grew.

7

Elizabeth Rosemond Taylor was born in London on 27 February 1932 of American parents. Her mother was a former stage actress and her father an art dealer. In 1939, a few months prior to the outbreak of war, the family moved to Hollywood, where her father opened an art gallery, much patronized by the film colony. The beauty of the owner's violet-eyed young daughter won almost as much praise as the paintings on the walls, and she was soon making her screen debut at the age of ten in *There's One Born Every Minute* at Universal. But it was M.G.M. who offered her a twenty-year contract, and cast her in *Lassie Come Home* (1943), *The White Cliffs Of Dover* (1944) and, most notably, *National Velvet* (1945).

Elizabeth's interest in the opposite sex goes back to the time when she developed a crush on John Derek, an older fellow pupil at a Hollywood school. Emerging into young womanhood, she dated football star Glenn Davis and R.K.O. boss Howard Hughes, but wedding bells rang for her and Nicky Hilton, the twenty-three-year-old playboy son of hotel magnate Conrad Hilton, on 6 May 1950. It seemed a fairy-tale romance, ideal fodder for the glossy fan magazines, as both were young, attractive, rich and pampered. M.G.M. took advantage of Hollywood's biggest wedding of the year by releasing *Father Of The Bride* (featuring Taylor as Spencer Tracy's daughter) at around the same time. After the marriage ceremony, she whispered to her mother, 'Oh, mother! Nick and I are one now, for ever and ever.'

'For ever and ever' turned out to be eight months. According to Elizabeth's testimony at the divorce proceedings, Hilton had ignored her during their long European honeymoon, drank heavily, and verbally abused her and her mother in public. He complained, 'I didn't marry a girl, I married an institution.'

The 'institution' was, in reality, only an eighteen-year-old girl. In due course she met the sophisticated British actor Michael Wilding, twenty years her senior, and fell in love with him. Wilding was in the process of ending an affair with Marlene Dietrich when Elizabeth, filming *Ivanhoe* in England, proposed to him. 'Elizabeth wants to be married to someone who will love and protect her and that someone, by some heaven-sent luck, turns out to be me,' Michael Wilding told the press after his wedding to Taylor on 21 February 1952 at a London register office. Her two sons, Michael Jr and Christopher, were both born by Caesarean section in 1953 and 1955 respectively. By 1956 the marriage began to totter. She was twenty-four, and becoming one of the most sought-after stars in Hollywood; he was middle-aged, set in his ways, and his career was fading. Clearly, the age gap which Elizabeth had insisted was unimportant at the outset played a part in the break-up of the marriage. 'It wasn't that we had anything to fight over. We were just not happy, and I think it was showing in the two boys,' Taylor remarked when they agreed to an amicable divorce. They remained on friendly terms until Wilding's death in 1979. Her floral tribute at his funeral read, 'Dearest Michael, God bless you. I love you. Elizabeth.'

Ironically, the man she was to marry next was five years older than Wilding but was noted for his youthful spirit and abundant energy. When Elizabeth met flamboyant impresario Mike Todd for the first time she thought, 'Oh! He's really quite good-looking for a producer.' Todd (real name Avrom Goldbogen), the begetter of *Around The World In Eighty Days*, wooed her in an extravagant and whirlwind courtship. At their wedding in Acapulco on 2 February 1957, Mike's lifelong friend, singer Eddie Fisher, was best man, and Eddie's wife, the popular Debbie Reynolds, was matron of honour. People close to the Todds were convinced that they were perfectly suited. 'Life with Mike is never dull. It's fun, more fun than I've ever had,' Elizabeth commented. In the same year their daughter Lisa was born, also by Caesarean, and both mother and child nearly died. She was advised never to have another baby. The proud father quipped, 'The baby is so beautiful, she makes her mother look like Frankenstein.'

A mere seven months later Todd's private plane, *Lucky Liz*, in which he was flying to New York, crashed in a storm near Albuquerque leaving no survivors. Elizabeth had wanted to accompany her husband on the flight but was persuaded to stay at home because of a flu virus. On hearing of the tragedy, she screamed so loudly that neighbours a few doors away could hear her. She had to be drugged to prevent her taking her own life. If death had not so tragically claimed him, thus allowing the entry of Burton into his widow's life, Todd would probably have remained the great love of Elizabeth's life.

Gradually, Elizabeth came out of seclusion and sought consolation in work (she completed one of her finest performances in *Cat On A Hot Tin Roof*, which she was already filming when Mike was killed), in her family, and also in the company of her late husband's friends, especially Eddie Fisher. They sat for hours together, talking about Mike and how much they missed him. Then, one day, as Fisher recalled it, 'Our eyes met and that was it. Not a word was spoken. I was in love with Elizabeth ... and I was certain she was in love with me.' By September 1958 they were involved in a huge Hollywood sex scandal. Taylor, who had been cast as The Grieving Widow, now found herself in the role of The Vamp who wrecked the Fishers' apparently idyllic marriage – a label that would be pinned on her again when Richard Burton left *his* wife for her. What the outraged moralistic public were unaware of was that the Fisher–Reynolds marriage was already in tatters, although they continued to play 'America's Sweethearts' because Debbie was pregnant with their son Todd (named after Mike) and they were worried that divorce would damage their popularity ratings. But on 12 May 1959, Elizabeth Taylor, who had converted to Judaism when she married Todd, married Eddie Fisher at a synagogue in Las Vegas.

When producer Walter Wanger announced that he was going to make a film called *Cleopatra*, he asked for Elizabeth Taylor for the title role. Twentieth Century-Fox executive Spyros Skouras favoured red-haired Susan Hayward, while Brigitte Bardot, Marilyn Monroe, Audrey Hepburn and Sophia Loren were also considered for the Queen of the Nile. Taylor wanted the part but she thought the script was appalling. When Wanger called her in London, where she was completing the interiors for *Suddenly Last Summer*, the star half-jokingly told him that she would do it for $1 million against 10% of the gross – and then only if there were drastic script changes and a foreign location. To everyone's astonishment, the studio agreed to her terms, making Elizabeth Taylor the highest-paid performer for a single film in the history of Hollywood, and setting a precedent for a handful of other stars in years to come.

Shooting on the picture began at Pinewood Studios on a cold English September day in 1960. Peter Finch was signed to play Julius Caesar and Stephen Boyd was to be Mark Antony, although neither of them was to see their leading lady for over a month. Taylor was first stricken with a cold, then a fever, then an infected tooth. As costs mounted, the temperatures dropped, and the cast and army of extras found themselves shivering in togas among the vast Egyptian and Roman sets.

In March 1961 Taylor was rushed to the London Clinic with lung congestion. For once the newspaper headlines were accurate: 'LIZ TAYLOR GRAVELY ILL': 'QUEEN'S DOCTOR CALLED'; 'LIZ SINKS'. She was given a tracheotomy which helped her breathing, but for days she was on the danger list. After some days in a coma she began to rally. Her physicians announced, 'She has made a very rare recovery. Miss Taylor is a woman of great courage. She put up a wonderful fight.' Since speaking was extremely painful, she wrote notes to Eddie, who was constantly by her bedside. 'Am I going to die, because I feel like I am?' she wrote. 'No, you're not going to die,' he replied. 'Everything's going to be fine.' She then scribbled, 'I love you,' and went into a deep sleep. She was later to comment, 'It was my subconscious which let me become so seriously ill.... Poor Eddie. My dream world which was Mike was much more satisfactory and much more real.' A Prince Charming was soon to wake the Sleeping Beauty from her dream.

In the spring Elizabeth won her first Oscar, after three consecutive nominations, for her role as a high-class hooker in *Butterfield 8*. Overnight she had regained the affection of the fickle industry and public. Shirley MacLaine, nominated for *The Apartment*, commented tartly, 'I lost to a tracheotomy.' As for *Cleopatra*, the entire project was shipped from the cold climate of England to sunny Rome. Rouben Mamoulian was replaced as director by Joseph Mankiewicz, who also wrote a new script. Finch and Boyd each made their exits, the former replaced by Rex Harrison. Wanger and Mankiewicz both wanted Richard Burton for the part of Mark Antony, despite Spyros Skouras' eccentric objection that, 'You can't understand a word he says.'

Burton's initial reluctance to play the role was dispelled by the prospect of being paid a quarter of a million dollars for three months' work. Most of it he earned sitting around in Rome with his wife Sybil and two daughters, Kate and Jessica, aged five and three respectively, while Taylor and Harrison enacted their scenes, which dominated the first part of the screenplay. Little did anyone suspect that Mark Antony's entrance would mark the beginning of a love affair to equal the historical immensity of the one they were filming. 'Of course, most of the literature on love

11

is complete nonsense. Those enormous, writhing love affairs that topple kingdoms and transform lives hardly ever happen,' Burton claimed before his own life was to be so radically transformed.

Richard Burton was born Richard Jenkins on 10 November 1925 in Pontrhydyfen, South Wales, the twelfth of thirteen children of a coal miner. Richard managed to get a scholarship to Oxford with the help of his school teacher and life-long friend Philip Burton, from whom he took his stage name. As he remarked later, 'I was chubby and short, spoke only Welsh, and had pockmarks on my face. Mr Burton took me and made something from nothing.' Years later, in recalling his childhood, Richard wrote significantly of an older sister who virtually brought him up. She was a 'green-eyed, blackhaired, Gypsy beauty' who had 'become my mother, and more mother to me than any mother could ever have been. ... It wasn't until thirty years later, when I saw her in another woman, that I realized I had been searching for her all my life.'

By the time Burton started acting during his brief spell at university he had already become what can only be called ravishingly beautiful. His looks went beyond mere handsomeness. He had also developed a speaking voice of uniquely melodious richness, and was acquiring a powerful charisma that allowed him to become the idol of the British theatre and, until he destroyed himself with drink and poor material, the cinema. He joined the R.A.F. in 1944 and, when he left it in 1947, he secured his first film role in Emlyn Williams' *The Last Days Of Dolwyn*. During filming he met Sybil Williams, a nineteen-year-old drama student who had a part in the picture. They were married a few months later in February 1949. Until Hollywood beckoned with a contract at Fox in 1952, Burton's energies were mainly concentrated on increasing his stage reputation, and he played many memorable Shakespearian roles at Stratford-upon-Avon and the Old Vic. Richard always had an eye for the ladies, but Sybil made sure he always returned to the nest. It never seemed to matter to her what he did; she would always say he was right, and never scolded him. He told a reporter, 'I shall never leave Sybil ... she thinks I'm a genius.' She said that her husband was 'wonderful ... making me feel people wanted to meet *me* equally'.

Around the time of the birth of his first child, Burton had an affair with nineteen-year-old Susan Strasberg, who was appearing with him in Jean Anouilh's romantic fantasy *Time Remembered* on Broadway. There were other sexual escapades. Joan Collins mentions in her memoirs how Burton made an unsuccessful play for her during the making of *Sea Wife* (1957). He told her that women always succumbed to him 'even if they were not receptive at the outset'. But he would usually inform his conquests that he would never leave Sybil for them. An actor friend commented that 'Sybil was patient, forgiving, perhaps preferring not to know more than she had to about ills she couldn't remedy.' However, she could never have been prepared for the impact Elizabeth Taylor made on her wayward but loving husband. 'I loved before. I loved Sybil in a different way,' admitted Richard in later years. 'I would say my love for Sybil was much more a love of a man for his daughter.... Before Elizabeth I had no idea what total love was ... I was shocked.'

Taylor arrived in Rome for *Cleopatra* with a large entourage consisting of one husband, three children, five dogs, two cats, various secretaries and dozens of servants, and settled at the Villa Pappa, a handsome fourteen-roomed mansion off the Via Appia, situated in the parklands around the studio. As it was only six months since she had returned from the dead, her health was of prime concern to everyone, not least the studio executives for reasons more mercenary than humane. Most solicitous of all was Eddie Fisher. He controlled his wife's diet and kept an eye on the amount of wine and cigarettes she consumed. 'I'm married to a woman who has to be loved and cared for,' he explained to reporters. Not far away, the Burton family were sharing a villa with Roddy McDowall, a friend of Elizabeth since *Lassie Come Home*, who was playing Octavius Caesar.

After the first 'electric scene' they performed together, Richard began frequenting Liz and Eddie's villa in the evenings. On one particular occasion, Richard regaled the guests with stories till one in the morning. Elizabeth was enthralled and laughed a great deal. Suddenly, Eddie went to the piano and started playing and singing loudly. An embarrassed hush fell over the company. Finally Elizabeth yelled, 'Shut up, Eddie! We can't talk!' whereupon the crooner slammed down the lid of the piano and strode into the next room. A few moments later, Eddie Fisher records were blasting through the house. Elizabeth covered her ears while the guests diplomatically left.

It was soon plain that Burton and Taylor were attracted to one another. 'I'm afraid at first it was lust, but then I got to know her and it was love,' Burton recalled. Elizabeth wrote, 'There was never any point at which Richard and I began. We just loved each other and there was no discussion of it. I mean it was there – a fact of our lives.... I really believe that whole lives can have turning points. When I came to, that last time [in the London Clinic], it was like being given sight, hearing, touch, sense of colour. Like I was, I don't know, twenty-nine-years-old, but had just come out of my womb. I knew that I wanted more in my life than what I had.' Walter Wanger also noted that 'When the day comes that she knows what she really wants from life, she will – I am sure – get it.' Certainly, what she wanted was someone with a stronger personality than Eddie Fisher, someone more reminiscent of the colourful Mike Todd.

When rumours of Liz and Richard's growing affection began to filter out from Rome to the world's press, the news was initially greeted with a good deal of scepticism. Since the earliest days of Hollywood, studio publicists had been feeding the public with tales of romantic liaisons between co-stars to stoke up interest at the box-office. As *Cleopatra* was a multimillion-dollar production, as well as one of the world's greatest love stories, what was more natural than to add a little spice to the P.R. material? However, the only spice that was taken was a pinch of salt. One Italian newspaper suggested that Elizabeth was really in love with Mankiewicz, and that Burton was merely being used as a decoy. The director laughed it off by declaring, 'The real truth is that I am in love with Burton and Miss Taylor is the cover-up for us.' Burton himself resorted to the old 'we're just good friends' line when answering questions on the nature of his relationship with his gorgeous co-star. Eddie Fisher insisted to gossip columnist Louella Parsons that 'The only romance between them I know about is between Mark Antony and Cleopatra – and that's a pretty good one. Elizabeth and I are still very much in love. We couldn't be happier than we are at this minute. We just have to live our lives and not let gossip interfere with the way we feel about one another. As long as Elizabeth and I believe in one another there never will be any truth to the stories.' Meanwhile Sybil Burton was claiming, 'I'm not going to live my life to please the press. I don't read newspapers, nor does my husband. I am happy and so there are no problems.'

Nevertheless, it soon became apparent that these collective protestations were very far from the truth. Jack Brodsky, Fox's assistant publicity manager, wrote to Nathan Weiss, his boss in New York, in February 1962 (part of their correspondence was later published as *The Cleopatra Papers*) that the affair 'started about three weeks ago and is now the hottest thing ever. It seems that Fisher found out about it and started squawking, so Taylor said, quote, I love him and I want to marry him, unquote.... Burton has told Taylor that he wants her too, but Wanger believes Burton will never leave his wife...'. A few days later Taylor was taken to hospital with a mysterious illness, and there was talk of a suicide attempt. Sybil left for London with the children. Eddie was in New York. After Elizabeth had recovered, he called her from America to ask her to deny the rumours that were circulating. She replied, 'I can't do that because there is some truth to the story.' Eddie hadn't counted on his wife's honesty, and the headlines shrieked, 'LIZ TURNS DOWN EDDIE'S OCEAN PHONE LOVE PLEA.'

The lovers tried to be as discreet as possible, but the *papparazzi*, Italy's notorious press photographers, watched their every move, often employing telephoto lenses to snap them together on private beaches. While on board an Italian publisher's yacht where Elizabeth and Richard were invited to Sunday lunch, she kept insisting that someone was taking pictures of them. Her instinct had been correct: newsreel and still cameras were discovered behind a curtain. 'She was living on the Via Appia Piatello and I was living on the Via Appia Antica,' Burton remembered, 'and though we were only about a mile away from each other, we couldn't get to each other without running the gauntlet of a thousand *papparazzi*. And I'm perfectly convinced that the phone was tapped.' Various ruses were used to put the press off the scent, such as having a man in drag leaving the villa in Taylor's limousine to be chased by *papparazzi*. But servants acted as spies for journalists, and journalists disguised themselves as servants to get a story.

Yet the celebrated couple often managed to foil the pack of publicity hounds that pursued them. Elizabeth revealed in the 1970s that 'Richard and I had some of the happiest times in Italy in a really crummy one-room apartment on the beach. We would go down there to be together even though we had a huge Roman villa with a cook and servants. We'd spend weeks there. I'd barbecue and there was a crummy old shower and the sheets were always damp. We loved it – absolutely adored it.'

Finally, weary of subterfuge, they decided to be seen publicly in the Via Veneto till the early hours of the morning, feigning indifference to the flashbulbs popping around them. 'LIZ AND BURTON FROLIC IN ROME; KISS, DANCE' drooled the headlines. It seemed to the press that Elizabeth Taylor was not only playing the most famous seductress of all time, she was *living* the role. The Vatican talked of 'this insult to the nobility of the hearth'; an Italian newspaper called her 'an intemperate vamp who destroys families and devours husbands'; Ed Sullivan on his television show said, 'You can only trust that youngsters will not be persuaded that the sanctity of marriage has been invalidated by the appalling example of Mrs Taylor-Fisher and married-man Burton.' Everybody was getting in on the holier-than-thou act. 'Good Lord, the reputations we had,' commented Burton. 'I mean I was a bestial wife stealer and Elizabeth was a scheming home breaker. You'd think we were out to destroy Western civilization or something.' Elizabeth, who had been there before when she married Eddie Fisher, said, 'I never felt dirty because it never was dirty.'

Joe Mankiewicz sprang to her defence. 'Talk about bum raps!' he exploded. 'Elizabeth is one of the least promiscuous, one of the least profligate beautiful women I have ever known. Perhaps if she had been more calculating and conniving – techniques more palatable to the morality mores she's reputed to have outraged – she'd have saved a great deal of wear and tear on herself.... Elizabeth is a good and generous and honest human being.' Five years later Lillian Gish, who worked with the Burtons on *The Comedians*, commented, 'They seemed the opposite of everything I had ever read about them. Elizabeth is a loving, devoted wife and mother. Even the animals preferred her when she came into the room. I told her that I might tell the truth about her, destroy her image, and ruin her career!' At the same time as 'Le Scandale', as Burton liked to call it, began to break, Taylor announced that she was adopting a nine-month-old girl called Maria. Three Caesarian sections had prevented her from taking the risk of giving birth again, and she worked for several months with the help of actress Maria Schell, after whom she named the child, to arrange the adoption. The baby had a crippled hip which several operations subsequently corrected.

The child was taken to the Villa Pappa where her new mother fed, bathed and changed her, giving her all the care, love and attention she needed.

Meanwhile 'we were all occupied, very seriously, in making a very serious picture', Mankiewicz related. 'The technicians worked under extreme difficulties within the cocoon of the sound stages. It was a tremendous strain, but we tried to leave the panic outside.' As filming neared its end, Burton and Taylor spent several weeks with Rex Harrison at his villa in Portofino, seeking some respite from the worst of the publicity. 'A man who comes through that ordeal of fire in Rome must emerge a different and better man,' Burton later explained. 'I sometimes wonder if I could go through it all again. I would have to – every pain, agony and torment of every moment. There was no choice then and there would be no choice now.' Taylor agreed. 'Yes, I'd do it all over again, with no provisions beforehand as to what would happen to me. You can't make provisions in life.'

Then, in the autumn of 1962, they decided to try a separation to 'get over' one another for the sake of the children on both sides. However, the families found themselves only about sixty miles apart in Switzerland; she and her children at her house in Gstaad; he, his wife and daughters at his villa outside Geneva. It was at this time that Elizabeth decided that, no matter what happened regarding Richard, she would divorce Fisher. Richard, though, was still infuriating her by telling reporters that he would never divorce Sybil. The first time this happened, Walter Wanger wrote that, in the scene where Cleopatra hears that Antony has gone back to his wife and she has to slash his clothes and bed with a dagger, 'She really went wild, lashing out in such frenzy that she banged her hand.' For Elizabeth love always meant marriage – and she had fallen deeply in love. Her children were a great consolation during this period. Seven-year-old Christopher told her that 'I prayed to God last night that you and Richard would be married.' A few weeks later, Burton and Taylor were in touch again, realizing that they would have to be together no matter what the consequences.

In November 1962 it was announced that they would make another film together. Originally titled *International Affair*, it was changed for moral reasons to *The V.I.P.s*. M.G.M. was longing to exploit the real-life situation, but had to play it down because, as one publicist remarked, 'Burton is, after all, still a married man.' Taylor and Burton decided to use the picture as an excuse to be together. For Elizabeth, the ideal relationship was one of equal partnership. She had managed to get Michael Wilding a contract with M.G.M. when she was there; she played an important part in Mike Todd's projects, and was about to star in his *Don Quixote* at the time of his death. She persuaded M.G.M to hire Eddie Fisher for a role in *Butterfield 8* and, many years later, she worked tirelessly on behalf of Senator John Warner. Now, with Burton, there seemed the possibility of a real joint career.

During the filming of *The V.I.P.s* in London, *Cleopatra* opened in New York in June 1963 to mixed reviews. The screenplay followed the plots of both Shaw's and Shakespeare's versions of the Egyptian queen's affairs with Julius Caesar and Mark Antony. After the elderly man–young woman relationship with Caesar, the Serpent of the Nile entwines herself round Antony, using her beauty, charm, wit and kohl-laden eyes to hypnotize him. Rex Harrison's performance as Caesar, which suffered less from cutting than the others, received the most critical approval. According to Taylor, 'They had cut out the heart, the essence, the motivations, the very core, and tacked on all the battle scenes. It should have been about three large people, but it lacked reality and passion. I found it vulgar. Yet I suppose I should still be grateful about having made the picture for obvious reasons.' Audiences seemed disappointed that the love scenes between Taylor and Burton that were the talk of modern Rome were not repeated with quite so much passion in those of ancient Rome. But public interest in their private lives still made the film the top earner of 1963 at $15,700,000.

In *The V.I.P.s* Burton and Taylor played a jet-setting couple on the verge of a marriage break-up, she torn between eloping with an opportunistic playboy (Louis Jourdan) and staying with her neglectful millionaire husband. The whole trite but glitzy tale takes place in and around London Airport where a variety of passengers are delayed by the fog. The starry-eyed pair pulled in the vast public, but it was the supporting cast, including Maggie Smith, Margaret Rutherford and Orson Welles, that gained the plaudits. While shooting the picture, Taylor and entourage were installed at the Dorchester Hotel. Burton occupied a separate roof-garden suite. He told a journalist in 1971 that 'apart from the fact that it was quite absurd, it meant it cost us double the money to live. ... In those days things were less permissive, so that there was all that fuss about separate rooms in hotels.' As Miss Taylor was earning a million dollars, and Burton half a million, for ten weeks' work, they could afford to pander to moral conventions.

Taylor joined Burton on location in Puerto Vallarta in Mexico while he was filming *The Night Of The Iguana* between September and November 1963. With only six-year-old Lisa to look after (the boys were with their father Michael Wilding in Los Angeles, and Maria was with Taylor's parents in London), Elizabeth was able to keep a close eye on her lover as he shot scenes with Ava Gardner, Deborah Kerr and eighteen-year-old Sue Lyon fresh from starring in *Lolita*. As usual the press hovered like vultures. 'Which leading lady do you think Mr Burton is going to make love to?' a boorish reporter yelled at Elizabeth. But most of the time they managed to avoid the prying eyes of newsmen, enjoying excursions round the area and going on fishing trips with John Huston, the film's director. Generally it was a happy time, except for one incident when Richard made Elizabeth weep by saying after a drinking session that 'the only thing in life is language, not love'.

However, Richard was still agonizing about what the end of his twelve-year marriage would do to his daughters, and continuing to tell reporters that he had no intention of marrying Elizabeth, while Sybil vainly hoped and waited for reconciliation. She told columnist Sheilah Graham that 'I would never allow the father of my children to become the fifth husband of Elizabeth Taylor.' In December, despite these bravado protestations, Sybil Burton finally gave up the fight and won a divorce *in absentia* in Mexico, claiming 'abandonment and cruel and inhuman treatment', and that her husband was 'in the constant company of another woman'. *Newsweek* called it 'the throwaway line of the decade'. Sybil began a new career in New York, where she opened a fashionable 'Swinging London' discotheque called 'Arthur' and married twenty-four-year-old pop singer Jordan Christopher with whom she subsequently had a daughter.

Elizabeth's divorce from Fisher was a more acrimonious affair as they wrangled over their extensive mutual holdings. In reply to accusations that his demands for a larger share of the grosses of *Cleopatra* was delaying Taylor's remarriage, Eddie told *Time* magazine, 'I wouldn't stand in the way of this earth-shattering, world-shaking romance for anything in the world. Legal matters take time and the great lovers will just have to bear up a few more days or maybe weeks. They stamp their feet, and if they don't get what they want, the world must stop! I don't condemn them for anything except trying to put the blame on me now. I'm just as anxious as Sir Richard the Lion-hearted Burton to get this thing over with.' Eventually, Elizabeth got her divorce in Mexico in March 1964 on the grounds of abandonment. (Eddie later married and divorced singer Connie Stevens.) Elizabeth Taylor and Richard Burton were free to marry at last. They had lived as man and wife for over a year, they had caused a scandal and split two families, but the public began to realize that they were deeply and genuinely in love, a love that had survived the many obstacles in their way. They could now continue to play The Great Lovers within a legal and moral framework.

They became the Burtons on 15 March 1964 – married by a Unitarian minister in a bridal suite at the Ritz-Carlton in Montreal. Elizabeth, wearing a pale yellow Irene Sharaff gown, and a $150,000 emerald and diamond brooch that Burton had bought for her at Bulgari in Rome, walked unescorted from one room of the suite to another where Richard was waiting for her. The bride and groom gave their respective religions as Jewish and Presbyterian, and the minister declared, 'You have gone through great travail in your love for each other.' After the ceremony Richard proclaimed, 'Elizabeth Burton and I are very, very happy.' They spent their wedding night in the suite and, according to Taylor, 'We sat and talked and giggled and cried until seven in the morning.' They then flew to Toronto where Burton was appearing in *Hamlet*. At the end of that evening's performance, after several curtain calls, Burton stepped forward and quoted a line from the play: 'We will have no more marriages.'

When *Hamlet* moved to New York, Elizabeth met her husband at the theatre after almost every performance, as crowds gathered to catch a glimpse of the world's most famous couple. Burton complained that he thought marriage would have reduced the public's interest by ending 'the somewhat illicit quality of our relationship'. In fact, although 'Le Scandale' was over, public interest in them only seemed to increase. They had rapidly become famous as celebrities rather than actors. 'I want to be known as an actress,' Taylor told the *New York Times* in 1964.

Unfortunately, their reputations as serious actors were not much enhanced by the next film they made together. *The Sandpiper* was a limp soap-opera played out against the gorgeous setting of Big Sur on the Californian coast. It concerned the love affair between a voluptuous, free-thinking, bohemian artist and a married Episcopalian minister. 'The dialogue was so awful, you'd die a little each day with embarrassment,' Burton recalled. 'We never thought it would be an artistic masterpiece,' Elizabeth said later. But despite the scornful reviews, and its growing notoriety as one of the world's worst films, box-offices were beseiged by crowds hungry to see its superstars.

All the while their marriage was being chronicled in great detail in fan magazines and newspapers. The public were told that Burton liked washing dishes as long as he was left alone to do it, and that he was tidier around the house than Elizabeth. 'As a housewife Elizabeth is highly naggable and limited,' Richard revealed. 'She is a good cook and makes marvellous breakfasts. I doubt if she can make a bed. When she cooks for an hour, it takes me four hours to clean up afterwards. ... Wherever we go, I insist on having a separate bathroom, if it's possible. Hers looks as if it has been hit by an atom bomb. ... But gradually Elizabeth has become more tidy than she was, and I've become less.'

Also meticulously recorded were what Taylor called the 'delight-ful screaming matches'. Throughout the 1960s their open quarrels earned them the nickname of 'The Battling Burtons'. Some of their affectionate banter on the film sets was along the lines of 'Does the burnt-out Welshman know his lines?' or 'Look at her. She walks and looks just like a French tart,' and Burton on Taylor's notorious tardiness, 'Isn't that wife of mine here yet? I swear to you she'd be late for the Last Bloody Judgement!' He objected to his wife's habit of swearing. In an interview Elizabeth announced, 'You know, I don't use four-letter words any more. Richard has broken me of the habit.' 'That's right,' Burton confirmed. 'I've cured Elizabeth of that unfortunate tendency.' 'You bet your ass!' she came back. 'That's a three-letter word,' Burton added without hesitation.

However, genuine admiration for one another came through in most of their comments. Burton continually claimed that Elizabeth had taught him how to act on film, teaching him that 'my very penetrating voice need not be pitched louder than a telephone conversation', and that film making was 'as exciting and as serious as playing Shakespeare on the stage'. 'Before I met Elizabeth I was making $175,000 a picture,' he declared. 'Now I'm making half a million. It makes you think, doesn't it? That girl has true glamour. If I retired tomorrow, I'd be forgotten in five years, but she would go on forever. She's a legend in her own lifetime.' For Elizabeth, Richard had 'widened my scope. He insists I be self-sufficient and independent. He introduced me to poetry, for instance, though I'd always been scared of it. I didn't think I could "say" poetry and he said that I was silly since I understood it.' She also said that he made her 'feel an intellectual equal of his, which of course I'm not'.

After the three less than convincing films the couple had made together, it was fortunate that their credibility as performers was soon brilliantly restored by *Who's Afraid Of Virginia Woolf?* in 1966. Initially, when producer Ernest Lehmann made the surprising offer to Taylor to play the bitter, fifty-two-year-old, frumpish, vulgar wife Martha, he did not consider Burton for the role of Martha's self-loathing professor husband George. But a determined Elizabeth persuaded an unenthusiastic Lehmann to cast Richard. He had intended to write a book while his wife was making the film, but 'Elizabeth started in on me, and those great eyelashes started to wiggle. ... ' A friend of Burton once claimed that 'It's the little lady who calls the shots,' and Burton admitted that 'virtually everything I've done in movies in the last three or four years has been Elizabeth's choice'.

Almost everyone on the picture had doubts about the project. When Elizabeth had first told Burton of the offer to play Martha, he retorted that she was at least fifteen years too young and far too beautiful for the part, but told her to take it 'to prevent any one else creating a sensation in it'. As shooting got under way, she wondered whether she had the acting resources to carry it off. Burton found it difficult to envisage himself in the role, and was worried about doing an American accent and playng such a weak man 'so over-run by that woman'. When Mike Nichols, the former television and nightclub comic and successful director of Broadway comedies, was hired to direct his first film, the industry was convinced that Warner Bros. would have a first-class turkey on its hands.

However, Edward Albee's hit play about a warring married couple opened to general acclaim in June 1966. Elizabeth Taylor, the legendary beauty, had been transformed, with the help of extra pounds, padding, and a tousled salt-and-pepper wig, into a blowsy virago, while Richard Burton, an heroic Hamlet and Mark Antony, was a whining, weary, bespectacled, hen-pecked husband. The picture was nominated for Oscars in all possible categories, and it seemed highly likely that a husband-and-wife team would carry off the top acting prizes for the first time in the Academy's history. It did not happen. When news of her winning her second Best Actress award reached her in Cannes, where she and her husband were shooting interiors for *The Comedians*, Elizabeth expressed anger and disappointment that Richard had not won an award as well. Burton, who had probably given his finest screen performance, never won an Oscar, although he was nominated six times.

Any suggestion by the press that the vituperative duelling of George and Martha in the film was a reflection of the Burton marriage was soon scotched by the pair's own words and actions. Richard told the *New York Herald Tribune*, 'Life with Elizabeth is like waking up and finding a wonderful new toy on your pillow every morning. You never stop marvelling or being surprised. I worship her,' and, 'I cannot see life without Elizabeth. She is my everything – my breath, my blood, my mind, my imagination. If anything happened to her I would die.' She was equally fulsome about him. 'If I'm away from Richard I feel like half a pair of scissors,' and, 'I love just reaching out in the middle of the night and touching ... saying "I love you" for no reason. I love more than anything else being married to Richard.' It was clear that they complemented as much as they complimented each other.

Following the completion of *Who's Afraid Of Virginia Woolf?*, the couple returned to England to appear on stage, without payment, at Oxford University for five sold-out performances of Christopher Marlowe's *Doctor Faustus*, the proceeds of which were to go to build an Oxford University Theatre Centre. Burton played the title role, while Taylor was the four-minute wordless apparition of Helen of Troy. 'All I had to do was kiss Richard and I know I do that well,' she commented. The couple also gave money towards the establishment of the National Theatre of Wales in Cardiff. Their limousines were often seen moving through the humble mining valleys of South Wales on their way to visit Richard's family. Just as Elizabeth had become Jewish because of Mike Todd, she now decided to give up her U.S. citizenship. The possessor of dual citizenship since birth, Elizabeth explained in 1966 that 'It's not true that I love America less but I love my husband more. ... I want to become British more than anything else.' In addition, she learnt to swear in Welsh.

The summer of 1966 saw them visiting Rome, the city where they first fell in love, to make *The Taming Of The Shrew*, thus repeating the roles that Douglas Fairbanks and Mary Pickford, the screen's other most celebrated married couple, had played over three decades earlier. At a news conference Burton told the assembled reporters, 'Gentlemen, now that we are respectable, I hope you will give us the same attention you did when we were unrespectable.' They couldn't get more 'respectable' than Shakespeare, although Taylor later recalled, 'I was so scared. It was the first time I'd tried to do Shakespeare. And my beloved was no help at all. "You do it on your own," he said.... But Richard did advise me, "Don't think of it as verse – don't pronounce it to a metronome as you were taught at school." And gradually I began to have fun with it.' Large audiences also had fun seeing the Burtons battling comically in Franco Zeffirelli's bustling, energetic and colourful film. Both leads suffered a multitude of bumps and bruises from the very physical action involved. In the knockabout situations, he had to be hit by her with a mandolin and have barrels thrown at him, while she had to be spanked by him over his knee. One thing Elizabeth refused to do for her role as the shrewish virgin, Katharina, was take off her wedding ring, so a pearl had to be sewn over it each day.

They co-starred in their following two films, *The Comedians* (1967) and *Boom* (1968), which allowed them to work in West Africa (standing in for Haiti in the former film) and Sardinia. For tax reasons, the Burtons could not film for more than four weeks in America, and therefore always insisted on foreign locations. Although both pictures came in for critical shellacking, the barbs did not seem to affect the glittering couple. All that mattered to them was working together and earning millions of dollars per picture to help finance their extravagant lifestyle. Even when Burton was playing Henry VIII in *Anne Of The Thousand Days* in 1969, Taylor had an unbilled part as a masked guest at a masquerade ball. Rumour had it that she was there to keep an eye on her husband who was supposedly involved with Genevieve Bujold, his young leading lady. But Burton insisted, 'I find it very embarrassing to work with any other actress after Elizabeth. ... I just don't enjoy kissing other ladies anymore. ... Since being with her I have never wanted another woman and I have never had another woman. When I married her it wasn't marriage to a big star, or someone who had been married three or four times before. What I was concerned about was whether I could stay faithful, because I had been a great womanizer.'

As the Burton circus moved from country to country, their way of life, which the *New York Times* likened to the court of Louis XIV, became ever more lavish. In the consciousness-raising late 1960s, younger people especially began to find them vulgar and frivolous and their films irrelevant. Elizabeth's eldest son would eventually become a hippie and live in a commune in Wales. The *Daily Mirror*'s headline read: 'LIZ'S DROPOUT SON; MICHAEL WILDING JR LIVES THE HIPPIE LIFE TO GET AWAY FROM ALL THOSE DIAMONDS.' 'Those diamonds' included the 33.19-carat Krupp diamond that Richard bought her for over $300,000 in 1968, a $1.5 million Cartier diamond set in a necklace of smaller diamonds, and the much-publicized heart-shaped diamond pendant Burton gave his wife on her fortieth birthday. The jewel, set in a gold mounting ringed with rubies and emeralds, hung on a diamond-studded gold chain made by Cartier. It was first given by Taj Mahal builder Emperor Shah Jehan to his young bride in 1621, engraved with the message 'Eternal Love 'Til Death.'

In fairness, the Burtons were equally generous in giving vast sums to worthy causes. Richard gave the equivalent of the Indian diamond's value to a British charity, and the United Nation's Children's Fund received as much as the cost of Taylor's extravagant fortieth birthday party in Budapest, attended by Princess Grace, Marlon Brando and Ringo Starr, among others. In 1966 Elizabeth established a heart disease research foundation in memory of her close friend Montgomery Clift and endowed it with $1 million. It would take pages to provide a full list of their many gifts to charitable organizations and individuals.

But all was not as well as it seemed on the surface. During the late 1960s and early 1970s, intimates of Burton began to realize that the actor had a drink problem. Why? He appeared to have everything – a wife he loved, millions of dollars, private jets, Rolls-Royces, homes in Mexico and Switzerland – and yet he would drink heavily like a man trying to dull a nagging pain within him. Perhaps it was his working-class Welsh puritanical background that provoked guilt – a guilt that was not assuaged by the large bequests to charity or the financial help he gave his family in Wales. When he was 'in his cups', which was often, he would mumble about the rotten films he was making, and rail against the jet set. There was also always a moment when he would speak about the unfulfilled promise of his stage career, his longing to play King Lear, and a desire to give everything up and lecture on Shakespeare at Oxford. But none of these things was possible as long as he was under the spell of Elizabeth Taylor. 'I'm like a bloke with a pimple,' Burton explained. 'He can't let it alone and I can't let *her* alone. I have to know she's somewhere around the house.'

The Burtons still retained their position as the most written about married couple on earth, despite a string of bad films, together and separately, and *Time* magazine's naming of them as 'the world's prize bores' in 1970. While Taylor's looks and performances still gathered praise, Burton continued to be an object of derision. Not untypical was the 1972 *Variety* review of *Hammersmith Is Out*. 'Burton', they wrote, 'goes through the film with a single bored expression. It's getting uncomfortably difficult to watch Richard Burton now without thinking of John Barrymore in his last days, parading the bleary remnants of a considerable talent through material at once third-rate and self-parodying.' This was of the man that influential critic Kenneth Tynan wrote, 'We thought he could be another Edmund Kean, that he was going to be the greatest classical actor living.'

In the summer of 1972 the couple decided to make a television film called *Divorce His: Divorce Hers*, a co-production between America's A.B.C. and Welsh Harlech TV to be filmed in Rome. Basically a good idea – a divorce as seen from the two different points of view of the participants – it was universally reviled. Typical was *Variety*'s 'It holds all the joy of standing by at an autopsy.' The filming itself had its problems, with Burton digging deeper and deeper into depression and the bottle, and Taylor continually arriving late to work. Waris Hussein, the director, told Paul Ferris, one of Burton's biographers, of an incident during the shooting of a night scene in an old side-street down which Richard had simply to walk and turn. 'Suddenly there was an uproar in the distance,' Hussein related. 'Hooting horns, a glare of lights, and she [Taylor] arrived, surrounded by police and *papparazzi*, in a black limousine. She got out wearing a black floor-length mink and said, 'Don't worry about me, Waris, I'll just stand in the corner and watch.' Meanwhile Richard had disappeared. When he was found, he was drunk and could hardly walk straight to do the scene.

On 3 July 1973, the eve of Independence Day, Elizabeth Taylor passed on a brief statement to the press which she had written on the stationery of New York's Regency Hotel. It read, 'I am convinced it would be a good and constructive idea if Richard and I separated for a while ... we have been in each other's pockets constantly, never being apart but for matters of life and death, and I believe it has caused a temporary breakdown of communications. ... I shall return to California where I have my mother and many true and good friends. Wish us well during this difficult time.' There was much speculation as to why the marriage was ending. Among a multitude of explanations given by a variety of sources were Burton's drinking, his roving eye, his 'temper and thunderous moods', according to Laurence Harvey, his declining career, her weight problem, her coarse vocabulary, and (unfounded) suggestions that she had had affairs with, among others, Warren Beatty, Helmut Berger, Roger Vadim, Peter Lawford, and Lawford's eighteen-year-old son. 'Maybe we have loved each other too much,' suggested Taylor.

In 1974 on television, Richard Burton said, 'I think that my life was changed by a woman who was called Elizabeth Taylor. I am not entirely sure what she did to me.' Aaron Frosch, Taylor's lawyer, told the press, 'The grounds will probably be incompatibility or some such moderate grounds. In other words it won't be adultery. They are very amiable, and no third party exists in either case. Also there are no financial issues to be settled. There is no hysteria, no name calling and no vilification. There are no issues, no problems, no squabbles. Now you're going to ask me why they're getting a divorce. All I can answer you is that I'm a lawyer, not a psychiatrist.' Peter Ustinov hazarded that 'they had been driven apart by the pressure of being the Burtons'. But they were never really able to extricate themselves romantically. Burton's 'Elizabethan years', as he later called them, were not over yet.

There were various attempts at reconciliation before the

divorce. In late 1973 Elizabeth entered the UCLA Medical Center to have her right ovary removed and an intestinal abnormality corrected. Burton, who was filming *The Voyage* in Rome opposite Sophia Loren, flew via London and over the Pole to be at his wife's bedside in California. For a few months they travelled the world together again. In the spring of 1974 she was with him in California where he was making *The Klansman*, but she soon left in what was described as 'an angry state'. It seems that Burton had given an eighteen-year-old waitress a ring. He explained that he had thought the girl would be perfect for a part in the film, and bought her a ring while choosing one for his wife. Few people were convinced. On 6 June 1974 Taylor divorced Burton at Gstaad, Switzerland. 'There were too many differences. I have tried everything,' she told the court.

After the shooting of *The Klansman*, Burton entered St John's Hospital at Santa Monica to try and dry out. He admitted later that at the time he was on to his third bottle of hard liquor a day, and had been given two weeks to live. He emerged after five weeks' treatment and went to Mexico to recuperate. He drank nothing but soda water, although he did start drinking a little again while rehearsing for his role as Churchill in the television play *Walk With Destiny*. Meanwhile Taylor had been seeing businessman Henry Wynberg, whom she had met through Peter Lawford. Burton started a relationship with Princess Elizabeth of Yugoslavia, the daughter of exiled Prince Paul, but the affair petered out, as did Taylor's, the reason being that the Burtons had got together again. 'We are stuck like chicken feathers to tar,' she commented.

They were reconciled in August 1975 and attracted as much attention as ever. The magic had not worn off after all these years. The fact that their love kept drawing them together was somethng the public recognized and warmed to. On a visit to South Africa in the autumn, an X-ray of Elizabeth's chest showed two spots on the lungs. 'I had about twelve hours to contemplate death,' she wrote, 'and a nasty one at that – cancer of the lungs.' Terrified, Burton and Taylor clung to each other all night, she gave him Valium and he whispered poetry in her ear. In the morning she was told that she didn't have cancer after all. In his joy, Richard proposed re-marriage. The ceremony took place on the banks of a river in Botswana. Remote as the area was, it was nonetheless invaded by swarms of photographers who materialized from the bushes. 'Without you, I was a ghost,' Burton told his bride.

In November a party was given at the Dorchester Hotel in London to celebate Burton's fiftieth birthday. Newspapers described him variously as looking 'shaky and lost' and 'like a man who wasn't there'. Photographs show him as pale, drawn, grey, and with large bags under his eyes. Elizabeth, however, at forty-four, appeared as glamorous as ever. It was inevitable that the second marriage was 'disastrous', according to Taylor, and a few months later they were again filing for divorce, which eventually took place in Haiti.

While Taylor and Burton were in Gstaad in January 1976, Richard met Susan Hunt, the twenty-seven-year-old wife of British racing driver James Hunt, in a ski-lift. They were married that summer. At the same time, Taylor met John Warner, former Secretary of the Navy to President Ford. He was a blind date arranged by a friend to accompany her to a Bicentennial dinner in Washington D.C. in the presence of Queen Elizabeth II. The other Elizabeth described her first impression of her date when he called for her at her hotel thus: 'He had his back to me, and all I saw was that marvellous silver hair. ... He turned round, "Ah, Miss Taylor." And I thought "Wow!" The 'Wow' was mutual, and Elizabeth became Mrs Warner in December 1976. The lives of Burton and Taylor seemed to have diverged for ever.

Elizabeth became a political wife, campaigning hard to get her husband elected to the Senate. She attended endless charity benefits and lunches, shook hundreds of hands, and spoke at public functions. But 'once he took office, there was little for me to do except attend teas and be presentable. It was so boring. That's why I put so much weight on. I was bored and eating all the time,' Elizabeth confessed. Burton, on the other hand, was allowing his new wife to run his business affairs, and much of his personal life. 'I was on the edge of self-destruction.... Susan saved my life. I met her just when I was putting my hand up for help for the last time,' he wrote in an *Observer* article entitled 'Lament For A Dead Welshman', ostensibly a tribute to his friend, actor Stanley Baker, who had just died of lung cancer. But, in spite of these loving plaudits, the marriage was over within a couple of years. Richard drank less and returned to the stage 'to discipline myself and to prove I actually wasn't the falling-down drunk'. Although his dream of playing King Lear came to nothing, his role of Dysart the psychiatrist in *Equus* on Broadway (repeated in the 1976 film) was a success. Elizabeth was in New York at the same time. One day Richard found scrawled on his dressing-room mirror in eyebrow pencil the words, 'You are fantastic, love.' It was his exwife's handwriting.

Taylor herself would tackle the Broadway and London stages in 1980 as vixen Regina Giddens in Lillian Hellman's drama *The Little Foxes*. She lost over forty pounds during a stay at a health resort, and her full beauty was restored. She was back in the show business limelight and revelling in it. The play became the hottest ticket in town, and received generally good reviews. It had been Burton and Taylor or Taylor and Burton for over four-teen years, now it was Taylor solo. With her career in full swing once more, Elizabeth was not content to be kept down on the farm in Virginia and, to few people's surprise, she and Warner divorced in 1982. Earlier she had created a sensation by appearing in several episodes of a daytime television soap called *General Hospital*, opposite a new beau, Tony Geary. He commented, 'Liz is a romantic. She needs a man around her. She prefers to be with a man rather than a woman. She has few female friends.'

In the same year as Elizabeth's divorce from Warner, the unsinkable double act of Burton and Taylor hit the headlines again. They would star together in Noel Coward's romantic comedy *Private Lives* on Broadway at a fee of $70,000 a week each. Sitting side by side at a press conference, they announced that Coward himself had suggested to them, during the filming of *Boom* (in which he played the Witch of Capri), that they should one day play the roles of Elyot and Amanda, the once-married and now divorced couple who meet up after five years while on their honeymoons. Each is married to a dullard (he, ironically, to a girl called Sybil), and they decide to run away together to Paris. 'We look like being in a hell of a mess socially,' says Amanda. 'Who cares?' replies Elyot. It seemed the perfect comeback vehicle for the fabulous duo. Naturally, there was speculaton that there would be another romantic reconciliation, and maybe even a third crack at marriage. It was just like old times. However, the media were not informed at the time of the production that both Elizabeth and Richard were involved with new companions: she with a Mexican lawyer, Victor Luna, he with Sally Hay, a film assistant.

The ticket prices for 'the theatrical event of the year' were the most expensive in Broadway history for a non-musical. At the

Boston try outs, people flocked to see the starry couple back together again as lovers, even if it *was* only on the stage. Sales dropped when the play opened in New York in the summer of 1983; the reviews were scathing, and news spread that they were both hopelessly miscast. But interest in them was as alive as ever, and every night fans crowded around the theatre to greet Elizabeth and Richard. During the run Burton married Miss Hay and reporters besieged Taylor, clamouring for her reaction. 'I'm thrilled and delighted for both Richard and Sally. I've known all along they would be married and happy together,' she told them. But when she fell ill a few days later, wagging tongues spoke of her depression over Burton's marriage. In fact, Taylor was suffering from a respiratory infection. Gossips also commented on Burton's absence from the 'Woman Of The Year' celebrations held in honour of Elizabeth at the Waldorf-Astoria. It was later learned that Richard, who had stopped drinking, wanted to avoid the temptation that such a banquet would offer him.

The curtain finally fell on the Burton–Taylor love story in August 1984, when Richard Burton died of a cerebral haemorrhage at the relatively young age of fifty-eight. Yet there was an epilogue. Burton was struck down at his villa in the Swiss village of Celigny where he was staying with his fourth wife, Sally. He was buried in the Welsh national colour of red as the words of Dylan Thomas's 'Do not go gentle into that good night' were spoken, and Welsh melodies echoed over the Swiss Alps. Elizabeth stayed away so as not to turn the funeral into a media circus. But a few days later she stood, stricken with grief, at the graveside of the man with whom she had shared the limelight for over two decades. Not long after, Elizabeth paid a visit to Burton's modest working-class family in Wales where she was greeted as their own flesh and blood. The press got wind of it and gathered outside the house. When Elizabeth came out she posed for photographers, this time without Richard at her side.

The fabulous couple that had enthralled the world for so long was no more. Apart from *Who's Afraid Of Virginia Woolf?*, the films they made together were 'the most unutterable rubbish', in Burton's own phrase, but the public didn't seem to care as long as the scenario of the real-life love story was exciting. After all, the world loves lovers, especially when they're larger than life. Richard and Elizabeth were certainly that.

NATALIE WOOD
— AND —
ROBERT WAGNER

The relationship between Natalie Wood and Robert Wagner constitutes one of the most remarkable – and one of the strangest – love stories to come out of Hollywood. Indeed, the facts read like a scenario for a Hollywood melodrama in which glamour, romance and passion bring happiness for a while, until the dream crumbles and sadness and disillusion set in. The middle section of the plot has the beautiful star embarking on a life of desperate but glossy promiscuity before she is saved by marriage to an older, protective man. Meanwhile, the male lead, who has been portrayed as something of a victim of his wife's glittering success, has quietly gone off and settled down with somebody new. Both second marriages, however, founder and, after a period in the wilderness for both of them, the young lovers of yesteryear meet again and discover that first love is best love. They re-marry, raise a family and, assisted by their hard-earned maturity, find the happiness, contentment and understanding that had eluded them in their youth.

The rich and famous female star spends more time now devoting herself to her husband and children than she does to making films; the good-looking husband rises to fame and fortune via television, which makes him a household name, but remains unspoiled by his status. The couple resolutely avoid working together so as to preserve the freshness of their private life. The arrangements suit everybody, the sanctity of a good marriage is emblazoned as a moral virtue, and the audience goes home uplifted.

So far, so good. But life, alas, is not like the movies. In reality, the complexities of Natalie Wood's life were writ large and, while she and Robert Wagner certainly did find true happiness the second time around, it was cut cruelly short by a devastating and unnecessary tragedy that killed Natalie at the appallingly early age of forty-three, leaving two little girls motherless and a husband racked with grief.

The couple's backgrounds could not have been more different. Wagner was born in Detroit, Michigan on 10 February 1930. His father was a wealthy industrialist and his son, whose clean-cut good looks and well-bred demeanour reflected his environment and his education, was destined for the business world. Somehow, he broke ranks and ended up in Hollywood, ambitious and very keen to do well as a film actor. In spite of a contract with Twentieth Century-Fox, however, Robert Wagner failed to achieve real stardom. He was excellent as the handsome, plausible psychopath in *A Kiss Before Dying*, but most of the films in which he appeared were unmemorable and his performances in them adequate but undistinguished. It was only many years later that he matured into a leading man of some weight, and the fame that he had sought came his way through several popular television series, notably the still currently successful *Hart To Hart* with Stefanie Powers cast as his wife and partner.

Wagner, nonetheless, was well known in the 1950s. It was an era when a certain kind of 'pretty', college-boy, good looks was fashionable, and this, together with Tab Hunter, Wagner possessed. He was also a charming, intelligent, well-liked young man-about-town, good fodder for the glamorous fan magazines. Legend, according to journalists, has it that Natalie Wood was infatuated with Wagner from a distance when, still a youngster, she saw him around the Fox lot and fell for his looks. It has also been reported that R.J., as he is commonly known, was first struck by the lovely young girl whose eyes, in the words of one writer, were 'as large and shining as a November moon' when she was twelve and far too young for him to consort with. He waited patiently, so the story goes, until her eighteenth birthday, whereupon he called her for a date.

By the time of that call in 1956, Natalie had made the transition from child actress to blossoming young adult being groomed for stardom. She was, in fact, one of the very few actresses who managed to bridge the gap successfully, Elizabeth Taylor being almost the only other notable example. In both their lives, the patterns of private insecurity pointed to the damage that was done by their abnormal upbringing. (Judy Garland, though she had been older than either of them when her career began, fared by far the worst, while huge stars like Shirley Temple and Deanna Durbin abandoned Hollywood when they grew up).

The dark-haired, dark-eyed beauty the world knew as Natalie Wood was born Natasha Gurdin in San Francisco on 20 July 1938. Her mother, who was given to exotic and conflicting accounts of her own origins, was certainly born of French and Russian parentage in China, while Natalie's father was a full-blooded Russian immigrant. They did not have much command of English, and Mr Gurdin made a living as a labourer. The family lived respectably, but hovering on the fringe of poverty, in the small town of Santa Rosa, California, where they might always have remained but for the chance visit of a film unit. Director Irving Pichel had decided to shoot location sequences there for a film called *Happy Land*, and sent out a call among the local population for extras. Mrs Gurdin, sensing an opportunity, took five-year-old Natasha along and the child was used. She made an impression on Pichel and, when he needed a child to feature with Claudette Colbert and Orson Welles (as Welles' adopted daughter) in *Tomorrow Is Forever*, he asked her to test for the role.

Mrs Gurdin, who wore the trousers at home, immediately packed the whole family off to Hollywood, not prepared even to entertain the thought that her daughter might fail the screen test. And, of course, she didn't. Irving Pichel, who became a lifelong friend, decided that her Russian name wouldn't do, so he anglicized Natasha and added Wood. So began a career, not only for Natalie, but for her mother. Mrs Gurdin very quickly emerged as the archetypal stage mother, dedicating all her energies and ambitions to pushing her daughter who, from the outset, was a 'natural' in front of the cameras.

The influence and control that Natalie's mother exerted over her should be noted, since the girl's upbringing quite clearly accounted for her later insecurities and temperamental difficulties. Until Natalie was in her mid-teens and a small spark of rebellion within her was finally lit, Mrs Gurdin virtually never left her side. She set great store by good manners, to the extent of training Natalie always to curtsey on meeting an adult; she discouraged the child from forming friendships, particularly with boys; she kept her schooling to a bare minimum, failing to see any virtue in formal education. Natalie's younger sister, Lana Wood, in her biography of the star, remarks that their mother believed that her daughters 'needed stardom or good marriages, preferably both'. Also, according to Lana, by the time Natalie had played her second little featured role in *The Bride Wore Boots*, it seemed clear that the girl was heading for stardom and 'From then on she was a commodity whose life was controlled by two forces, her mother and her studio.'

Tiny, pretty, talkative and mischievous, for ten years or so Nat, as she was sometimes called, played several nieces, a couple of sisters and the odd neighbourhood friend. She also played daughter to, among others, Maureen O'Hara (*Miracle On 34th Street*); Gene Tierney (*The Ghost And Mrs Muir*); Margaret Sullavan (*No Sad Songs For Me*); James Stewart (*The Jackpot*); Fred McMurray (*Never A Dull Moment*); Bette Davis (*The Star*). It was during the filming of *The Star* that a lurking fear of Natalie's came to the surface. One scene required her to jump off a boat into the ocean and swim, but she was terrified of the water and put up a prolonged and emotional protest until the compassionate intervention of the great Bette Davis (who would remain Natalie's ideal of a superb actress) convinced the director to use a double. In view of Natalie's terrible death by drowning, the story has acquired a chilling irony.

After the making of *The Star*, even Natalie's mother couldn't keep her from full-time schooling any longer, and the girl was given two years off from filming to attend high school and complete her patchy education. These were very happy years for Natalie, who flourished in the company of her peers, enjoying the routines of a normal teenager and taking an interest in her studies at which she did well. The family was by now, of course, financially stable, and Natalie, who adored all animals passionately, was able to keep a collection of them at home. Home was reasonably spacious and comfortable and boasted a swimming-pool, but her mother neglected the house and family disgracefully, occupying herself as 'lady-in-waiting to Natalie the star'. Father, through his wife's efforts, was employed at Twentieth Century-Fox studios. He had started as a carpenter but had worked his way up to a position in the special effects department.

Natalie's period at high school brought her her first taste of personal freedom. Her independent will that had been crushed into submission by her mother and the demands of her career finally began to assert itself. This led to periodic rows at home, but she didn't give in and Mrs Gurdin, whose opposition to the idea of Natalie dating boys bordered on the neurotic, was forced to loosen the ties a little. The girl was occasionally permitted to go out unchaperoned, and was allowed to entertain friends at home by the pool as much as she wished.

By the time of her high school graduation Natalie Wood had grown into an undeniably beautiful young woman. She was very much a modern American girl but she was already noted for her fastidious make-up, grooming and dress. All of her life her public image would be that of a perfect clothes-horse, beautifully turned out to give her a glamorous outer surface. By the 1970s her appearance contrived to give her a curiously dated image, more like the gracious ladies of an earlier era, and, together with the clutch of remarkably poor films in which she starred, contributed to her box-office decline. In 1955, however, she was a very saleable commodity and her first significant break came when she was cast opposite James Dean in *Rebel Without A Cause*. The success of that film needs no comment, but if it made Dean the most famous youngster of his generation, it did no harm to Wood's status, particularly as she received her first Oscar nomination for her performance.

Warner Bros. signed her to a long-term contract and set the star-building machinery in motion. She responded well: after all, most of her young life had been spent in long hours of hard work and, as a consequence of always having been surrounded by adults, she had developed poise, a deft social manner and – professionally at least – confidence. The studio cast her as a white girl who has been kidnapped and brought up by Indians in John Ford's superb revenge Western, *The Searchers*. This led to a succession of half-breeds in far less distinguished films and, although she was kept busy, it can't be said that she was making a major impression as an actress.

On the personal front, Natalie enjoyed a close friendship with James Dean and with Sal Mineo, who had also featured in *Rebel Without A Cause*. It is disturbing to note that both these young men met premature and violent deaths, as would Natalie. The actress dated Nicky Hilton, the hotel millionaire's son who was

Elizabeth Taylor's first husband, and, strange to relate, took up with Elvis Presley. That relationship was one of the briefest in history. They had only just met when the singing idol took her to his family home for the weekend. Two days with Elvis' mother was enough for Natalie. She fled. Then, in 1956, she began dating one of the film colony's handsomest young bachelors, eight years her senior and very eligible. ...

Robert Wagner's courtship of Natalie Wood was conducted in the true Hollywood tradition. They made a ridiculously attractive pair, and wherever they went the photographers and the columnists followed. It is a little cruel but probably true to suggest that fame came their way more for their public romantic aura than on the strength of their limited professional achievements. R.J. proposed to Nat on 6 December 1957, and no girl could have wished for a more fairytale beginning. He arrived at her parents' home bearing a bottle of champagne and a pair of crystal glasses. The drinks poured, Natalie drained her glass to find, nestling at the bottom, a beautiful pearl and diamond ring engraved with two words, 'Marry Me.'

The wedding took place three weeks later at Scottsdale where Wagner's parents lived. That the young couple were very much in love was evident and their nuptials were thankfully free of Hollywood ballyhoo. They honeymooned in Florida, travelling by train because the nineteen-year-old bride had a fear of flying. In fact, beneath her composed exterior, the young Mrs Wagner was prey to a host of fears and, within a year or two, like so many actresses, she would need sleeping pills to ward off the demons of insomnia, and in 1966 she made a suicide attempt. Meanwhile, she learned to mask her feelings with the odd brittle wisecrack. When, for example, she was talking to a reporter, she quipped, 'Sure I'm domestic. I can call room service.'

The couple bought a house in Beverly Hills and trumpeted as Hollywood's perfect and beautiful couple, they expended a disproportionate amount of energy trying to live up to the ideal. That they sported wardrobes full of designer clothes was one thing; Natalie's ambitions regarding her home were another. She longed to express herself through the creation of beautiful and, in contrast to her mother, orderly interiors, but her inexperience led her into pretensions that proved disastrous. She attemped to convert their home into some sort of classical Grecian temple

but, three building contractors and a lot of money later, succeeded only in creating what *Time* magazine called 'a Pompeiian
extravaganza'. It was almost absurdly ornate, and so badly con-
structed that a ceiling collapsed on to the vast, canopied marital
bed. Wagner himself observed much later, 'We tried too hard to
live like glamorous movie starts of the past.'

In 1960, during their third year of marriage, Wood and Wagner
co-starred in a feature film for the first and last time in their
careers. *All The Fine Young Cannibals* was a witless and forgettable farrago that did nothing for either of them. In Natalie's case
this was not too serious. She had worked a great deal having,
among other things, taken the title role in *Marjorie Morningstar*
opposite Gene Kelly, appeared with Frank Sinatra in *Kings Go
Forth*, and co-starred with James Garner in *Cash McCall*. She was
bright enough to know that her material was letting her down,
and sufficient of a tough, professional star to refuse the next poor
script offered her after her film with her husband. What, in fact,
she did go on to do was play Maria in the successful screen
version of the Jerome Robbins–Leonard Bernstein musical *West
Side Story*, which won six Academy Awards.

For Wagner, however, prospects were rather less bright. He
had spent almost more time on the golf course than in the film
studios, and such work as he had done was unmemorable. An
ambitious, intelligent man and, as time would show, a competent
actor, he nonetheless seemed unable to shift his stagnating
career. As so often happens in show business partnerships, the
unequal balance of professional standing between husband and
wife was placing a severe strain on the marriage.

The situation came to a head when Natalie was filming *Splendor
In The Grass*. Her co-star was a still relatively unknown but
indescribably handsome young man named Warren Beatty who,
for three years or so, had been dating Joan Collins. When it
became obvious to Miss Collins that Beatty was not the marrying
kind, she set sail for her home country of England. At around the
same time, Robert Wagner arrived in London to do some filming.
Meanwhile, as Natalie and Warren enacted the passionate love
scenes for *Splendor In The Grass*, it was apparent that the
electricity between them was more than just fiction. The couple
began to go out together and were soon one of the choicer items
for Hollywood gossip. Needless to say, the rumours reached

Wagner in no time at all and, in one of those incestuous arrangements common among film stars, he spent time escorting Joan Collins in Europe. In April 1962 the marriage which had so captured Tinseltown's hardened imagination and promised so much happiness was formally dissolved.

Within a year of his divorce from Nat, R.J. married again. His new wife was Marion Marshall, a blonde actress who had previously been married to director Stanley Donen by whom she had two young sons. Robert Wagner thus acquired a ready-made family, to which he and Marion soon added with the birth of their daughter, Kate. The second Wagner marriage seemed solid enough and lasted for seven years; it is not really clear why it, too, ended in divorce.

For Natalie, life ran a rather different course. Warren Beatty, famous for preserving his independence within a relationship, broke his own rules and moved in with his new love. It was a tempestuous affair, punctuated for Natalie by enormous, exciting highs, and terrible, depressing lows. They were together for a little over a year, until Natalie no longer had the strength to weather the storms of their differing temperaments.

Natalie went into analysis. She took it very seriously and seemed heavily dependent upon it, never missing her daily consultation even if it meant holding it by telephone from her studio dressing-room. Within a few years, she declared that her therapy had been completely successful in sorting out her problems and helping her to confront her true self. She moved house often, steadily developing her longed-for flair for creating a beautiful home. Her dedication to her work was exemplary and, when filming, she would diet almost excessively, stop smoking, exercise rigorously and sacrifice the evening cocktails which she happily admitted to enjoying.

Her career certainly continued to be active. She was teamed with numerous top box-office male stars such as Steve McQueen (*Love With The Proper Stranger*); Tony Curtis (*Sex And The Single Girl; The Great Race*); Robert Redford (*Inside Daisy Clover; This Property Is Condemned*). But in some strange way, Natalie Wood's star status was something of an illusion. The films she made were largely mediocre, and her own work came in for a deal of negative criticism. While recognized as competent and eminently watchable, she was accused of being cold, mechanical, hollow and one-dimensional, The famous *Harvard Lampoon* instituted the 'Natalie Wood Award for the Worst Performance by an Actress' and berated her, somewhat unfairly, for offering 'saccharine, whining caricatures of American girlhood'. In 1968 the show-biz 'bible', *Variety*, analyzed her output and implied that she was not worth the vast sums of money she was paid.

Throughout the seven years till she met and married her second husband, Natalie Wood's life was a merry-go-round of dates, infatuations, affairs and engagements. Her escorts ranged from the highly eligible, including David Niven Jr, Robert Evans and Arthur Loew Jr, to the marginally unsuitable. Then Richard Gregson entered the picture. An Englishman who had moved on from being a very successful London agent to involving himself with film packaging and production, Gregson was much older than Natalie, a man of worldly sophistication who exuded an air of confidence. In spite of the superficial glitter of Natalie's existence, she was lonely, and vulnerable to the prospect of a secure marriage. Gregson fell in love with her, and she appeared to reciprocate his feelings.

Natalie Wood and Richard Gregson were married in 1969 in a full and lavish Russian Orthodox ceremony, surrounded by celebrities and well-wishers. Her family was delighted with the turn of events, and she herself seemed happy in the love and protection of a man she clearly respected. The new Mrs Gregson brought a serious approach to her marriage that the young Mrs Wagner of twelve years earlier had been ill-equipped to do. She went into semi-retirement (although she made one of her best films at this time, *Bob And Carol And Ted And Alice*) to concentrate on home and husband and, most importantly, pregnancy. In September 1970 Natalie's greatest dream came true when she gave birth to her daughter, Natasha. The adored baby became the centre of Natalie's existence. She was a wonderful mother and the household revolved around Natasha's needs.

The demands of Richard's work often took him away from home, but Natalie's loneliness during his absences was relieved by frequent phone calls from her husband. Sometimes she took the baby to their holiday home at Lake Tahoe and all in all, for Natalie, basking in her husband's affection and the joy oj mother-hood, life seemed to have worked out at last. She was not, however, an eastgoing woman. Her childhood had left its emotional scars and she was complex, hypersensitive and easy to anger. She was often humourless and, while quick to apportion blame to others if she were hurt or angry, she was also relentlessly unforgiving. When, therefore, she had reason to suspect Richard of infidelity, she would not listen to any explanation. She threw him out and, when her mother and her sister Lana tried to stop her from making a hasty and irrevocable decision, she regarded that, too, as a form of betrayal. Not much more than two years after they were married, therefore, the Gregsons were divorced and, except for Natasha, Natalie was alone once more.

A couple of months later Robert Wagner's divorce from Marion, from whom he had separated a year earlier, was finalized. By now he had not only matured as a screen personality but the international fame which for so long had eluded him had begun to come his way through his television series *It Takes A Thief*. For a time his name had been heavily linked with Frank Sinatra's second daughter, Tina, but by early 1972 the romance was over. Natalie's relief from post-divorce depression was to go out with her old friend Steve McQueen, who was himself just divorced from his long marriage to Neile Adams and not yet involved with Ali MacGraw. By the time she made an unbilled cameo appearance in *The Candidate*, as a favour to her friend Robert Redford, Natalie was deeply unhappy. She was looking ravishing, and had her adored child to care for, but she was alone, her career was going nowhere, and she was seeing her analyst. Looking at her in a more optimistic light, she was free of encumbrances – and so was Robert Wagner.

The couple had, in fact, met again for the first time in many years some months before Natalie's parting from Richard Gregson. They had each – in the full knowledge that the other would be present – accepted an invitation to a dinner party given by mutual friends. Richard was away on business and Natalie was, therefore, on her own. Naturally the initial encounter was awkard, full of painful memories of the past which was not, contrary to appearances, dead and buried for either of them. Later that evening they sat in a corner and talked intently for a long while. They were re-establishing a friendship but, when the evening was over, they quite properly went their separate ways. When Nat's second marriage collapsed, R.J. waited a decent interval and then called her.

It didn't take long for the gossips to detect that the couple were wining and dining together rather frequently in the sort of cosy, intimate restaurants to which lovers are always drawn. But the gossip remained whispered on the private circuit until the objects of it decided to go public. They did this by choosing to go together to Hollywood's single most glittering and renowned occasion, the Academy Awards ceremony. That night in 1972 when they stepped out of a shared limousine was a night to remember. The photographers went wild, the newspapers nationwide gave coverage and indulged in speculation, their fans were hysterical with sentimental delight. Could it really be ... ?

The dream, worthy of a Ruritanian musical fantasy, came true on 16 July 1972 when, for the second time, Hollywood's 'beautiful couple', Natalie Wood and Robert Wagner, were married. They exchanged their vows in the golden glow of a Californian sunset, aboard a fifty-seven-foot yacht anchored off the coast. The ceremony was as private as their courtship had been public, with only their families, their closest friends and their respective daughters present. The happiness of the occasion was palpable, and the bride had never looked more radiantly lovely or the groom more distinguished and handsome. They honeymooned on the yacht, alone, sailing up the coast to Catalina. Soon they would buy their own yacht, *The Splendor*, and repeat this journey many times before the sea claimed Natalie's life.

Nat and R.J. settled down in a graceful and opulent New England-style mansion in Beverly Hills. This time they got it right. He had impeccable taste, she had a wonderful sense of colour, and they were both free of the silly pretensions of fifteen years before. They created a beautiful home where Natalie was content to play wife and mother and welcome her husband after his day's work at the television studios. They co-starred in a couple of television dramas: *The Affair* in 1973, *Cat On A Hot Tin Roof* with Laurence Olivier, who later became a friend, in 1976. But the most important event in their lives was the birth of their daughter, Courtney Brooke Wagner, in March 1974.

That these two people had found each other again and rekindled their first love so successfully is a remarkable as well as a romantic story. Nat's father, Nicholas Gurdin, told a reporter that, in his view, 'Their first break-up came because they were two kids, impetuous and obviously immature. But now things are different. They're two mature people, coping with reality.' Wagner has said, 'Natalie was my first real love, as I was hers, and I think once you've had that kind of marriage or relationship with your first love, that feeling never really leaves you. You always feel something special for that person.' Natalie, who regarded their second chance as a stroke of immense good fortune, expressed similar sentiments but, perhaps most interestingly of all, revealed that during their years apart, 'We were always inquiring about how the other one was, and caring what was happening to the other one. But always ... the timing was never right. This was the first time that both of us were free at the same time.'

Mr and Mrs Wagner had nine and a half years of true happiness. There was no sense of Natasha being an outsider with her step-father – mother, father and two daughters were a united and affectionate family unit. Work sometimes took R.J. away from home, but more often than not he was around, an attentive and generous husband. He patently adored his wife, whom he showered with gifts, and to whom he was particularly supportive on the now infrequent occasions when she worked. They spent many quiet evenings relaxing alone at home, but they also enjoyed entertaining. It all seemed too good to be true, and the Fates, who had given them their second crack at happiness, decided to intervene.

On 29 November 1981 the beautiful Natalie Wood met her death by drowning. At the time she was making a film called *Brainstorm*, and she and R.J. decided to spend the couple of days she had off just after Thanksgiving on board *The Splendor*. They had invited Nat's co-star, Christopher Walken, to accompany them. On the fateful evening the little party took the yacht's dinghy across to Catalina where they were dining at a local restaurant. They consumed enough champagne to give the restaurant's manager a twinge of worry about their return journey, and he called the Harbour Patrol to keep an eye on the dinghy when they left. The Wagners and Walken, however, arrived back without mishap, climbing aboard at about 10.45 p.m. A nightcap was suggested, but Natalie opted to go to bed, leaving the two men to drink and chat.

According to Lana Wood in her biography of her sister, Natalie was always 'wise enough to go to bed when she'd had too much to drink – and she often did. She was tiny, so it didn't take much, and she liked her white wine.... When she had had enough of the party, of the wine, of whatever, she would leave.' In other words Lana, who was devoted to her sister, makes it clear that Natalie couldn't hold her liquor. That night, when she went off to bed, she was behaving true to form and there was no foundation for the ugly and vicious rumours that she was having an affair with Walken, that he and Wagner quarrelled and that, somehow, these events were responsible for the star's death.

What, in fact, was revealed by the investigations of experts was as follows. Natalie's efforts to sleep were disturbed by the dinghy banging against the side of the yacht because it had not been properly secured and, in her hazy state, she got up to attend to it. She pulled on a down-filled jacket over her nightgown to protect herself from the cold wind, and this proved to be her undoing. When the jacket became saturated with water, it also became very heavy, which meant that Natalie had to strain against a weight that was constantly pulling her down into the water during her struggles to reach the shore. When she untied the dinghy it blew away, she reached out for it and fell overboard. By now the wind was violent and she was swept out to sea, from where her cries for help went unheeded. She fought hard to stay afloat, contending with the alcohol, with the weight of her jacket, with the elements – and with her own terrible fear of the water. The single most horrible fact about the tragedy is that she actually came within two hundred yards of the beach before she was pushed into unconsciousness by the combination of fatigue and the freezing water.

The appalling loss of Natalie Wood sent waves of genuine shock and grief through the Hollywood community. She had, after all, spent thirty-eight of her forty-three years as a prominent member of that community. Created by the now extinct studio system, she represented the last active vestige of old Hollywood, and there could never be another like her. The personal loss to her husband and children was, of course, incalculable. Robert Wagner has survived the ordeal through his devotion to his children, helped by a natural love of life, sheer strength of character, and the support of understanding friends. One of the most important of these was the actress Jill St John. They shared an intimate relationship which ended because, in the final analysis, his love remained with Natalie.

Perhaps the purest tribute to the love between R.J. and Nat is in the words he spoke when asked by a journalist whether he was trying to exorcise the past. He replied, 'Who would want to exorcise the past? You cannot, and I wouldn't want to try. Who would want to do that with all the wonderful memories of life?'

HUMPHREY BOGART
—AND—
LAUREN BACALL

've heard you're planning to use a new girl in the film,' said Humphrey Bogart to Howard Hawks, who was about to direct Bogie in *To Have And Have Not* (1944).

'I'm going to try something,' Hawks replied. 'I'm going to try and make a girl as insolent as you are.'

'Fat chance of that,' said Bogart, grinning.

The 'new girl' was a nineteen-year-old fashion model whose photograph Hawks' wife Slim had seen on the cover of *Harper's Bazaar* over breakfast one morning, and shown to her husband. Hawks was immediately enraptured by the picture of the beautiful, auburn-haired, almond-eyed girl posing in a black Mata Hari costume, and invited her to come to Hollywood for a screen test. She was a New Yorker named Betty Perske, an aspiring actress of virtually no previous experience. Hawks worked for months on her appearance, personality and acting, and got her to lower her voice considerably to a distinctive, sexy husk.

'When you look at a man, study him so that he wonders what the hell you're thinking,' he advised.

This lowering of the head and raising of the eyes became known as 'The Look'. With her name changed to Lauren Bacall (although she would insist on always being called Betty), she was ready to face her co-star. At their hasty first meeting neither was terribly impressed. The forty-four-year-old Bogart, who even as a young man was never much attracted to young women, found her 'a very long girl'. In high heels Betty was a shade taller than the five feet nine inch tough-guy star. She had had visions of playing opposite glamorous leading men like Charles Boyer and Tyrone Power and thought to herself, 'How awful to be in a picture with that mug, that illiterate. He won't be able to think or talk about anything.'

Altogether it seemed an unpromising combination on screen – never mind off it. Not only was there a vast disparity in their ages, but they came from widely differing backgrounds. Far from being a rough diamond, he was the son of wealthy blue-blooded Dr Belmont DeForest Bogart and renowned magazine illustrator Maude Humphrey. Betty was born into an extremely modest Jewish home in the Bronx, the only daughter of William Perske, surgical equipment salesman, and Natalie Weinstein, housewife. The thrice-married Bogart, one of Warner Bros.' highest paid stars, was a hard-drinking cynic, while Bacall was unworldly, shy and drank only rarely.

In fact, all the differences became unimportant after they had worked on the picture together for a few days. On screen it was a rare pairing of equals. Her Slim (named after Mrs Hawks) had, according to the critic James Agee, 'a fierce female shrewdness, and a special sweet-sourness ... she manages to get across the toughest girl Hollywood has dreamed of in a long, long while'. She was also called a 'Bogart in skirts'. Memorably she utters the lines, 'You don't have to act with me, Steve. You don't have to say anything or do anything. Maybe just whistle. You know how to whistle, don't you, Steve? You just put your lips together and blow.' By the time that scene was played Bogart and Bacall had fallen in love and were about to become a legend in the chronicles of Hollywood romance.

As filming progressed the relationship between them developed and grew ever more intimate. The chemistry that worked magically on screen was only a mirror image of the feelings they had for each other off it. Betty found that, in contrast to his film persona, Bogie was a sensitive, intelligent and widely read man. Knowing of his love for boats, she quickly learned to sail in order to share his pleasure. He realized she was wise far beyond her years, and they shared the same sense of humour. At the time, his third marriage was heading for the rocks, and Bacall was his lifesaver. Betty was the exact opposite from the woman to whom he was married.

Bogart had been married for six years to a forty-one-year-old petite blonde actress called Mayo Methot. They fought on their drunken wedding night, and continued doing so for the rest of their marriage. Mayo was an alcoholic and, under her influence, Bogie changed from being a moderate drinker to a heavy one. She was also given to violent outbursts and insane jealousy of every woman her husband played opposite. Until Bacall came along she never had any cause. One of the reasons offered for Mayo's resentment was her claim that she had given up her career for Bogart. The truth was that Mayo, in spite of appearing in small roles in over twenty films, never had much of a career to give up. She got little pleasure from Bogart's increasing fame, calling him 'that cheap little ham actor'.

Bogart's previous two marriages, both to actresses, had been equally unsuccessful. His first wife was a talented redhead named Helen Menken whom he met in 1924 (the year of Bacall's birth) when they were both starting out in the theatre. They lived together for two years before marrying, but eighteen months later were divorced after Helen charged that Bogart beat her. It was not long before Bogart had entered a second marriage, confidently stating, 'I had enough women by the time I was twenty-seven to know what I was looking for in a wife the next time I married.' She was Mary Philips, an actress he had worked with on stage. When he was offered a Hollywood contract in 1930, Mary refused to give up a role on Broadway to go west with him. When Bogart returned nearly two years later without having lit up Tinsel Town, Mary admitted to having fallen in love with an English actor Roland Young while on tour. She gave Young up and Bogart determined never to be separated again from his wife if he wanted to remain married. When he was given another bite at the Hollywood cherry in the role of gangster Duke Mantee in *The Petrified Forest* in 1936, Bogart took Mary with him. While he was making a name for himself as a heavy at Warners, Mary became restless for the stage, and accepted a part in New York. Bogart was furious.

'This is the first time I'm really able to support you,' he said. 'We could never afford to have children before. Stay here and let's start a family.' His pleas went unheeded, Mary returned to the east coast, and they were divorced in 1938. Later that year Bogart married Mayo.

During the shooting of *To Have And Have Not* Bogie promised Betty that it would not be long before he would obtain a divorce from Mayo and they could marry. But it was not as simple as it sounded. Mayo was capable of doing violence to herself and to others. She had once tried to stab Bogart, and had cut her wrists. He also suffered a certain amount of guilt and pity for Mayo, whom he was deceiving. After the day's work Betty would return to the small apartment she shared with her mother, and Bogie to his house and Mayo. The situation was unbearable for the lovers, who needed to be together. Betty seldom went out, hoping that Bogie would be able to telephone her from a call-box, or even find an excuse to leave his house and pay her a visit. Sometimes Betty's mother would go to a film in order to leave them alone, or they would eat at a drive-in or in the car at the beach. So intolerable did the clandestine situation become that Bogart decided to take a chance and move out, but Mayo threatened to kill herself and he moved back.

Finally, after many months, Bogie convinced Mayo that their marriage had no future, and they were divorced on 10 May 1945, with Mayo receiving a generous settlement. Eleven days later Humphrey Bogart and Lauren Bacall were married at the large farmhouse of his novelist friend Louis Bromfield in Ohio. Twenty-year-old Betty had to have a parent's signature to get the licence. The wedding was held in the great central hall of the farm with hundreds of press people swarming around. The bride wore a rose-beige doeskin suit with brown accessories and a gold whistle around her neck – a present from Bogie, inscribed, 'If you want anything just whistle.' The groom wore a grey tweed suit and black elevator shoes. During the ceremony, in which the word 'cherish' was substituted for the word 'obey' at Betty's insistence, Bogie wept continuously. The couple spent their wedding night in a large bedroom suite at the farm, and their honeymoon on the train back to Hollywood.

On the face of it there seemed every reason why the marriage would not last. There were Bogart's three failed marriages, his steady drinking and, most of all, the twenty-five-year age gap. Commenting on the latter Bacall said, 'The age difference thing is a lot of crap anyway. There is twenty-five years' difference between us and we get along pretty well, mostly because he tolerates some of the things I talk off about, like politics. I think he's happy with me and I don't take credit for it. Bogie's a wonderful husband. I'm certain I could look far and wide and never find a husband as good as he is.' Unlike Bogart's other three wives, Betty brought him complete understanding and sympathy. She was his buffer against the world and, in contrast to Mayo, helped him cut down on his alcohol consumption.

Both Humphrey Bogart and Lauren Bacall were very different from how the public perceived them on the screen. The gruff, tough anti-hero was a sensitive, insecure man who read Plato, Emerson and Shakespeare. He also hated violence. As dandified actor Clifton Webb, a friend, explained, 'He's not a tough guy, not at all. He's about as tough as Little Lord Fauntleroy.' The sexy siren was a domesticated woman, who liked cooking and keeping a tidy and comfortable home. 'I always wanted a career,' Bacall told biographer Joe Hyams, 'but I also wanted a home of my own, a husband and children. I made up my mind long ago that when I did find them they would come first. If my career interferes with our domestic life, it's best that I give it up.' In fact, that is what she subsequently did.

So passionately in love were they that they couldn't bear to be parted for more than three or four hours. Whether they were working on different pictures or on the same one at Warner Bros. they would travel to work together every day, and meet during the coffee and lunch breaks. After work whoever finished first would wait for the other so that they could share the drive home. During the making of a film they were usually in bed before ten at night and up before six in the morning but about once a week they would dine at Romanoff's or LaRue's Restaurant on the Sunset Strip where they would dance to 'their song', 'That Old Black Magic.'

When John Huston, who had just directed them both in *Key Largo* (1948), the last of their four films together, cast Bogie in *The Treasure Of The Sierra Madre* to be shot on location in Mexico, the star insisted that he would only do it if Betty came along. 'Without her, I'll be miserable,' he told Huston. 'We got married to be together, and that's how it's going to be.' Bacall added that a wife belongs with her husband. Huston agreed to her going, as he did four years later when Bogie was making *The African Queen* in the Congo.

Although there was never any reason for either to feel or display jealousy, they were inclined to be extremely possessive and protective of one another. One night Bogie cut in when Betty was dancing too closely with the Shah of Iran. He seemed to have little fear that his wife would fall for the charms of a younger man. 'Betty likes older men,' he pronounced. 'She finds older men much more entertaining. She is tremendously interested in knowledge and finds the young ones a little callow.' He did, however, tell Betty that if she met anyone and wanted to take off, then she should come and tell him as he hated anything dishonest. There was no chance of that! Betty, on the other hand, knew that her husband was not a ladies' man, despite his three previous marriages. He was only interested in one woman at a time, and the time was now hers. Nevertheless, she had to sometimes take women to task at parties for making too much of a fuss over him. 'Bogie dislikes scenes and he has no heart for the chase anyway, so the problem of other women doesn't exist,' she said with confidence. And contrary to many a Hollywood marriage, there was hardly a whiff of scandal surrounding theirs. Bacall's only rival was Bogie's boat *Santana* which he bought from Dick Powell. She tried as much as possible to share his love of the open sea, but was prone to seasickness and disliked the long stretches in a confined space. But she knew how important the boat was to him, both as a hobby and as therapy, so she never complained as long as she knew when he would return to land.

The only things missing to make their marital bliss complete were children. Bogie started to have hormone treatment, the sole result of which was the hastening of the balding process. Thereafter, he wore a series of toupeés in his pictures. Finally, in 1948, Betty informed her husband that she was going to have a baby and a few nights later, at a dinner given by Harry S. Truman, Bogie bet the President twenty dollars that it would be a girl. In January 1949, after Stephen Bogart was born, Truman received a twenty-dollar bill, which he signed and returned to Bogie to keep as a memento. At the age of forty-nine Bogart was overjoyed to be a father for the first time, and his happiness was complete when, three years later, Betty provided him with a baby girl called Leslie (named after Leslie Howard).

The Bogarts became part of the Hollywood aristocracy, entertaining lavishly in the fourteen-room French Colonial house in Benedict Canyon which they bought from Hedy Lamarr. Bacall was a wonderful hostess. As John Huston commented, 'She was adorable to Bogie and his friends and she was always warm, charming and dear. ... She was in love with him and he with her, and anyone who liked Bogie liked her. They were a joy to behold together.' It was remarkable how the girl from the Bronx adapted so easily to Hollywood high-life at a very young age. This was mainly due to her upbringing by her mother, who had divorced Mr Perske when Betty was four. Natalie Weinstein changed her name to Bacall, the Rumanian for wineglass as Weinstein was in German, scrimped and saved to dress her daughter well, send her to a good school, and give her ballet and drama lessons. While still at school young Betty modelled pre-teen clothes, and played truant to go and watch Bette Davis films, some of which featured Humphrey Bogart. Now she had been up there on the screen with him, and was his wife.

In 1953, after three years' absence from the screen, a period dedicated to her husband and children, Betty found it difficult to refuse a co-starring role in *How to Marry A Millionaire* with Betty Grable and Marilyn Monroe, the old and new blonde sensations at Twentieth Century-Fox. At the same time, Bogie went off to make *Beat The Devil* in Italy. They were apart for four and a half months, the longest period of separation of their marriage. Lonely and miserable without his wife, Bogie, not usually much of a correspondent, wrote to her every day. The fact is, he could seldom relax or be himself without her beside him. Despite her otherwise benign influence on Bogie, Betty was never able to get him to reduce his alcohol or cigarette consumption below a level that was not a risk to his health. At the time he was filming *The Barefoot Contessa* in 1954, he would wake up each morning with a hacking cough. Although he cut down on his drinking and smoking, the cough continued.

Sometimes Bogie would criticize Betty for making the few films she did, instead of concentrating her energies on him and the children. Although she would defend her career choices, Bacall knew how depressed Bogart would be when he returned from the studio and she was not at home, and that he felt instinctively that his time was running out. During the shooting of his last film, *The Harder They Fall*, he would complain of how tired he was after a day's work. 'I don't know what's the matter with me,' he said. 'I don't seem to have any pep any more. Old age is catching up on me, I guess.' Bogart was fifty-seven.

Towards the end of 1956 the couple had signed to make their first film together in eight years, a comedy to be called *Melville*

Goodwin, U.S.A. Just before shooting Bogie visited his doctor with a pain in his throat. The doctor immediately advised an operation to remove a cancer of the oesophagus. 'Can't we make the movie first?' Bogie asked. 'You can make the movie first,' replied the doctor, 'and you'll be a big hero at Forest Lawn.' Betty was with her husband in the hospital all the time, sleeping on a bed beside his. Although the growth was removed, Bogie returned home still in great pain, looking sickly and underweight. Betty, who knew that he did not have long to live, hid her grief by being her own cheerful self around him and his friends. Acknowledgement of his imminent death never crossed Bogie's lips. He spoke of the future he would enjoy with his adored children, his boat and new film projects. Propped up in his wheelchair, he would receive his close friends in his den, among them David Niven, Frank Sinatra, George Cukor, Richard Burton, John Huston, Spencer Tracy and Katharine Hepburn.

On 13 January 1957 Tracy and Hepburn paid him a visit. When they leaned over to say goodnight, Bogie said, 'Goodbye, Spence. Goodbye, Kate,' instead of goodnight. He was not the only one to have a premonition. Betty decided to spend the night on the bed with him. Humphrey Bogart died at 2.10 the next morning.

Humphrey Bogart faced illness and death with exemplary courage. Alistair Cooke published an eloquent obituary in which he commented that Bogart was '... a man with a tough shell and a fine core.... By showily neglecting his outward forms of grace he kept inferior men at a distance.... From all of them he was determined to keep secret – the rather shameful one in the realistic world we inhabit, of being a gallant man and an idealist'.

'When Bogie died, the bottom dropped out of my life,' Bacall said. At the age of thirty-three she was alone but for young Stephen and Leslie. Betty had lived with her mother until her marriage, seldom dating other men. During her eleven years with Bogart they were rarely away from each other. He had been everything to her. For some time after his death she remained in the house surrounded by reminders of him. She kept his clothes, slept in the bed they had shared, and visited the hotels, restaurants and other places where they had been happy together. Only gradually did she come to realize that she could not live in the past for ever, that she had to make a new life of her own. She sold the house and began working again. She was seen out with Frank Sinatra for a while, and there were rumours they might marry, but it came to nothing. Around Christmas 1959 Betty met Jason Robards Jr, who resembled Bogart not only physically but in his humour and his liking for Scotch whisky. It was obvious that in marrying Robards in July 1961 Betty was hoping to recreate her idyllic relationship with Bogie.

Since her divorce from Robards in 1969 Bacall has never contemplated marriage again. The memory of Bogie still continues to dominate her life and career. She has become part of the Bogart cult that has grown to immense proportions since the mid-Sixties, and is proud to be still considered the grieving widow of one of the great men of cinema.

MARILYN MONROE
— AND —
ARTHUR MILLER

In July 1960, a film unit left for locations in Nevada where in the experienced hands of John Huston they were to begin shooting a black-and-white drama called *The Misfits*. The screenplay had been written by one of America's most accomplished and respected playwrights, Arthur Miller, as a homage to the fragile and elusive nature of the film's leading lady, his actress wife Marilyn Monroe. By the time filming commenced, however, their marriage was in shreds.

The Misfits, an elegiac piece, became a literal elegy to three major Hollywood stars. Clark Gable, the leading man, died of a heart attack eleven days after shooting was completed and this closed an important chapter in Hollywood history. Montgomery Clift, the other major male star, died five years later when he, too, suffered a heart attack, bringing his tormented life to an end at the age of 45. The leading lady died within eighteen months of the film's release, from an overdose of barbiturates. She was only 36. It was not a surprising end, considering her history of insomnia, pill dependency and hospitalization, but the tragedy was nevertheless shrouded in mystery, speculation and sinister allegations which continue to the present day.

Marilyn Monroe was born Norma Jean Mortensen on 1 June 1926. This is one of the few facts of her life that was never in dispute. For the rest, she herself variously edited and embroidered her muddled past for the benefit of the vast Hollywood publicity machine which she instinctively knew could create her in her own desired image. So dense was the morass of half-truths, contradictions, fantasies and downright lies that it was many years before it was discovered that Maurice Zolotow's authoritative biography of the star had served to perpetuate them. It wasn't Mr Zolotow's fault. He was no sensationalist; he merely collected together the subject's own accounts of her life that included, among her more lurid fabrications, the well-known 'fact' that she had been raped at the age of eight.

Nobody writing of Marilyn Monroe now should attempt it without reference to *Norma Jean*, a biography written in 1969 by Fred Lawrence Guiles. Mr Guiles has provided a thorough, non-partisan and painstakingly researched account of Marilyn's life in which he has sought to sift fact from fiction, to unravel the mystery, debunk the myth and clarify the phenomenon that was Monroe. It makes fascinating and depressing reading, and helps us to trace the path that led her to Arthur Miller, the great love of her life, who came as her saviour only to be reduced to a piece in the puzzle of her destruction.

To speak of Miller as Marilyn's great love is not entirely accurate. Certainly, her devotion to him, while it lasted, was the strongest she had shown to a man, but the tragic truth is that Marilyn's only true love was the camera. To the camera her devotion was total, her trust in its power absolute. The camera raised her to her status as an incomparable icon of sexuality and vulnerability and, in the end, destroyed her with its demands. A capricious god that bestows its favours on few, the camera had chosen Garbo as its legendary creation, and remained loyal to her until its eye lit upon a rather ordinary (as Garbo had been) working-class American factory worker who, in surrendering to its possibilities, was transformed from Norma Jean Dougherty – she had already married Jim Dougherty – to the limpid beauty desired by every man in the world. She almost obliterated the memory of Jean Harlow and Clara Bow; she sent Garbo to the museum of ancient memory; she eclipsed the potency of the fabulous Rita Hayworth. In front of the camera, Marilyn Monroe had everything, gave everything, and never betrayed it.

But, ultimately, there was little comfort to be drawn from the camera because Marilyn's end was in her beginning, which brought her into the world with a legacy of madness that would cast a dark shadow over her own identity for the rest of her life. Norma Jean's mother, Gladys Mortensen, was a Hollywood studio film cutter. Her first husband was called Baker and she had two children by him. (Marilyn is sometimes erroneously documented as having been born Norma Jean Baker.) They divorced and the children went to live with their father in Kentucky. Gladys then married an itinerant workman of Norwegian extraction named Edward Mortensen but by the time Norma Jean was born he had left his wife. Nonetheless, he was to all intents and purposes the father of Gladys' child, and it was not until many years later that Marilyn discovered she was the illegitimate daughter of a good-looking film salesman named C. Stanley Gifford, who left Los Angeles to become a successful dairy farmer. In her young adulthood Marilyn decided to make contact with him, only to be cruelly rebuffed. Gladys was a fragile, pretty woman who worked hard, was shy and reserved and had few friends. Her own mother, Della, had been twice married and Gladys was the daughter of her first husband, a Mr Monroe from whom Marilyn would take her new surname. Della's marriage to Monroe had ended when he was committed to an insane asylum. She, too, was of unstable temperament and shortly after Norma Jean's birth was institutionalized. When Norma Jean was seven Gladys suffered a severe mental breakdown and began the cycle of hospitalization which would prevail for most of her life.

For the first couple of months of Norma Jean's life Gladys was a caring and devoted mother but the task quickly proved too taxing for her limited resources. The baby was sent to live with a kind, industrious and God-fearing couple, Ida and Albert Bolender. Gladys visited her daughter regularly and moved in with the Bolenders to nurse her when she was ill, but her presence only contributed further to the child's confusion as to who her parents actually were. She got on reasonably well with the Bolenders' other foster child, Lester, but when they officially adopted the little boy she sensed a subtle change in her position and, justifiably or not, felt less loved and wanted.

Gladys had always dreamed of being able to have Norma Jean back. She saved hard and was finally in a position to put down a payment on a pleasant white bungalow near the Hollywood Bowl. In the autumn of 1933 she moved her daughter, now seven, into the house but, in order to make ends meet, she leased the entire premises to an English couple and rented back a couple of rooms for her own use. The Englishman earned his living as a stand-in for George Arliss; his wife was a film extra. The new régime constituted not only a major upheaval in Norma

Jean's life but a major change in her environment. She found herself in a world of grown-ups, not of the church-going kind to which she was accustomed but people who passed their evenings at cards while sipping scotch and bourbon. On Saturdays the little girl would be deposited at the cinema where she would happily spend the afternoon, sitting through the feature three times whenever she could. Her love affair with the glamorous unreality of Hollywood's dream world began that year in the darkness of Graumann's Egyptian and Chinese Theatres.

The new order soon collapsed. Gladys, in spite of her sense of achievement in housing her daughter, found herself unable to cope with the realities of daily contact and responsibility. She suffered increasing malaise and unhappiness and, in January 1934, she broke down one morning when her daughter was at school. Apart from a short period over a decade later, Gladys and Norma Jean were parted from that day on. Gladys was diagnosed a paranoid schizophrenic and committed to a state asylum. Norma Jean, returning from school on that bleak January day, was told that her mother was ill and in hospital, and that was all she would know for many years.

The English couple, helped by financial contributions from Gladys' best friend Grace McKee, looked after the child for almost a year until they were forced to abandon the house. Some neighbours, Mr and Mrs Harvey Giffen, took Norma Jean in, and Los Angeles County took over financial responsibility for the child, appointing the loyal and kind Grace McKee as her guardian. The Giffens grew extremely fond of the girl and, when they decided to move back to Mississippi, wanted to adopt her. But Gladys, ill as she was, adamantly refused to surrender her child. Another similar offer from old friends of Gladys, which at least would have kept the girl in California, was also turned down. And so, at the age of nine, Norma Jean Mortensen was placed in the Los Angeles Orphans' Home Society where, on arrival, she had to be forcibly dragged inside, screaming with all the pain and damaged pride of her young life, *'I'm not an orphan!'*

The orphanage was no bleak Dickensian repository of cruelty but a rather graceful semi-colonial-style building, reasonably comfortable, and run with humanity and understanding as well as discipline. Nonetheless, an orphanage it was, with all the drabness of existence that implies. In the twenty-one months she spent there Norma Jean never came to terms with being a member of an institutionalized group; she felt lonely and isolated and clung to any small signs that she was noticed as an individual. The quest for love and admiration and recognition had begun, and that often involved retreating into a fantasy world.

Norma Jean's discontent worsened and she and a friend tried to run away from the orphanage. Her guardian, Grace McKee, realized that something had to be done and organized a brief series of foster homes for her, beginning in the summer of 1937. Grace, meanwhile, married Doc Goddard, gaining not only a husband but three stepchildren. When Norma Jean's unhappiness at her current foster home was so severe that she asked to be sent back to the orphanage, Grace and her husband finally decided to give her a home with them. Thus Norma Jean grew into adolescence against a background of reasonable comfort and security. She entered junior high school, went to the cinema as much as she could, and formed what proved the longest and happiest association of her life with Grace Goddard's aunt, Ana Lower. Miss Lower was educated, comfortably off and a dedicated Christian Scientist, and a bond of real affection sprang up between this middle-aged woman and the growing girl. Over the years Marilyn would stay with Ana on occasion, and would often turn to her for comfort and for guidance. Meanwhile, she had a companion, both at home and at school, in Doc Goddard's daughter Beebe, who shared her passion for films.

Encouraged by Grace, Norma Jean began dating the handsome, eighteen-year-old son of the Goddards' friends and neighbours, the Doughertys. In the spring of 1942 the girl dropped out of school and, on 19 June that year, only a couple of weeks after her sixteenth birthday, she married Jim Dougherty in a conventional ceremony, and became the houseproud mistress of her own little home. The accounts of how Marilyn became a bride for the first time are colourful, sometimes a little bizarre and, in details, contradictory. What emerges as absolutely clear is that Grace, who was moving to West Virginia with her family, was plunged into uncertainty as to what to do with her ward. Jim Dougherty was a responsible, clean-living young man who earned a good wage at the Lockheed Aircraft Company, and Norma Jean seemed to think him attractive. He appeared to be a suitable prospective husband for the girl and, certainly, a marriage would solve the problem of her immediate future. Accordingly, Grace put her best energies and her will into engineering the match, and the young couple found themselves married almost without realizing it was happening.

The marriage, however, was not by any means unsuccessful. Jim took care of his young wife and grew to love her. They were good companions and compatible lovers and, if she was sometimes bored and lonely during his absence, she valued his kindness and the real security he seemed to offer her. Norma Jean was, however, playing her first major role, that of proud housekeeper and loving wife, and as she changed and matured it was inevitable that the fantasy would run its course and she would have to move on. They had been married for two years when Jim went overseas with the Navy. His wife went to live with her in-laws and, to alleviate her restlessness, took a job at a defence plant where she packed parachutes, then moved on to spraying fuselages. She threw herself into the work with dedicated zeal, earning the respect of the bosses and the hostility of her fellow workers. She wrote dutifully and lovingly to Jim, but he was becoming a distant memory and a present constraint.

Photographer David Conover appeared one day at the Radio Plane Company to compile a photographic essay for *Yank* magazine on women in war work. He picked out Norma Jean Dougherty to model for him and unwittingly began the creation of a legend. Not only did she prove a 'natural' in front of the camera but her whole personality expanded into vivacity and assurance; she responded to direction; she made valuable suggestions; she loved the camera, and it loved her in return. Conover showed the pictures to his friend Potter Heweth, who asked the girl to pose for him for some colour transparencies. He, in turn, took the exciting results to a lady by the unlikely name of Emmeline Snively, the head of a successful modelling agency. She immediately wrote to Norma Jean, suggesting that the girl might find an occupation more rewarding than the aircraft factory if she cared to learn about modelling.

The following week Norma Jean took sick leave and presented herself to Miss Snively. She also moved out of her in-laws' house and went to stay with Ana Lower. She remained at the factory for a short while, then abandoned it to pursue her new career full-time. Effectively, at the age of nineteen Norma Jean Dougherty departed this world and Marilyn Monroe, aspiring star, entered it. The rest of her life would be a struggle between these two identities which created a constant split in her psyche. The damage done came nearest to being repaired ten years later in the care of Arthur Miller but by then, alas, it was too late.

The internationally acclaimed playwright Arthur Miller, whose Pulitzer Prize-winning *Death Of A Salesman* is a modern classic, was born into the teeming streets of immigrant New York in 1915, although he was not the slum child that description generally implies. His father, Isidore, was a reasonably well-to-do clothing manufacturer, and Arthur was schooled in the Jewish tradition and its values of self-improvement. The family security, however, was shattered by the Depression in October 1929 when Isidore Miller, along with many thousands of other Americans, went to the wall financially. The humiliation, as well as the poverty, caused by those terrible years left an indelible mark on Arthur Miller's thinking, and shaped a view of life that informed his plays and coloured his political sensibilities. The latter, of outspokenly liberal hue, led him to the House UnAmerican Activities Committee, before whose interrogations he refused to bend his principles, and the State Department withheld his right to a passport. By that time, however, Miller had worked his way through the University of Michigan, scratched a living by freelance writing, and returned to his beloved Brooklyn where he settled into his first marriage and fathered two children. He had also become famous.

As Guiles comments, '... When Arthur Miller first took a magnifying glass to the American social scene, a couple of things were at once evident. Here was an often brilliant analyst of American mores and an equally gifted auditor of the American idiom, but an uneven writer of prose ... two of his plays, *Death Of A Salesman* and *The Crucible*, have the evocative power and mercilessly clear focus to rank him as a writer of importance and permanent value.'

The tall, lean, craggy, bespectacled writer met the blonde, curvaceous film star during a visit to Hollywood in 1950. After a fleeting introduction at the film studios, they saw each other again at a party where they talked intently in a corner for hours, during which discourse he was enquiring, attentive, sympathetic and easy to be with. It is clear from all accounts, including her own, that Marilyn fell in love with Arthur that night. She rushed home and told her dramatic coach, Natasha Lytess, with whom she was staying, 'It was like running into a tree. You know – like a cool drink when you've got a fever. You see my toe – this toe? Well, he sat and held my toe and we just looked into each other's eyes all evening.' It is said that thereafter, except during the period of her second marriage to Joe DiMaggio, Marilyn slept, like an infatuated schoolgirl, with a photograph of Miller under her pillow, but she showed uncharacteristic restraint in respecting his marriage and did not try to interfere.

But the fire had been kindled for Miller, too. He returned to New York and a marriage that, while not exactly unhappy, had gone stale with the years. As soon as he was home, he wrote Marilyn a long letter in which, among other things, he said, 'Bewitch them [the public] with this image they ask for, but I hope and almost pray you won't be hurt in this game or ever change.' Caring words which were to become redolent with sad irony. Marilyn had told him that she longed for someone to admire, a figure to fill the gap created by her fatherless background. Miller suggested, 'If you want someone to admire, why not Abraham Lincoln? Carl Sandburg has written a magnificent biography of him.' Marilyn, who was a voracious reader and self-improver, acted on his advice and became a friend of the eminent Sandburg whose book inspired her to admire *him* more than his subject. This is one of many circumstances that gives the lie to the popular image of Monroe as a dumb blonde.

Over the next three years Monroe and Miller corresponded, spoke on the telephone from time to time, and met in New York on a couple of occasions. Whatever the strength of their feelings might have been, the relationship remained, on the face of it, merely a friendly one, and one which was to be interrupted for a while by Marilyn's new lover. Baseball player Joe DiMaggio was America's favourite sporting hero. His fame was almost as great as his future wife's, even if it did carry a somewhat different aura. He was old-fashioned, conservative, shy, and simple in his tastes, although he had a passion for wearing beautiful clothes. He was very much a man's man, and valued his privacy while enjoying his renown. Entirely devoid of any artistic or intellectual pretensions, DiMaggio considered the denizens of the film jungle greedy phonies, and the image of dignity which he pursued was to be severely ruffled by marriage to the world's number one sex symbol. The public display of her physical attributes offended DiMaggio's notions of propriety and, ultimately, provoked a jealousy and resentment that he was unable to bear.

Meanwhile, Joe fell very much in love with Marilyn whom he met early in 1952. It was a long courtship, punctuated by quarrels, and she had difficulty making up her mind to marry him. They enjoyed an excellent physical relationship but had not much else in common, and it took her until January 1954 to become Mrs Joe DiMaggio amidst a fanfare of publicity. The marriage lasted a mere ten months, its final disintegration occurring during the filming of the famous scene in *The Seven-Year Itch* when the draught from a grating blows the star's skirts up. Daring stuff for 1954, and DiMaggio found the whole spectacle of the location shooting insupportable. In the final episodes of Marilyn's life, however, it was Joe who rallied round as her trusted friend, protector and sometime lover.

By the time Marilyn Monroe met Joe DiMaggio she was one of the most talked of and written about women in the world. She had travelled a tough and sometimes ignominious road to reach her position, always driven by her own fanatical determination to succeed. To her, of course, success was not merely a matter of fame: success was thought to be a passport to love, adulation, security and, above all, respect. It was to be the magic panacea, or so she believed, that would erase the miserable memory of Norma Jean. For years, however, she was regarded as little more than amusingly decorative – as Darryl F. Zanuck, against whom she was very bitter, put it in a studio directive at Fox, she was to be written into any picture that required the presence of a sexy blonde. And she was. At Fox, at M.G.M., at Columbia, all of whose executives failed to spot her potential, she was fobbed off with a succession of supporting roles in mediocre films.

It was through the good offices of Emmeline Snively that she had got her small start in films. Under Snively's guidance she became a successful and much noticed magazine cover-girl, whereupon Emmeline put her in touch with an actors' agent, Harry Linton, and engineered her some useful publicity. Linton worked hard for her, but it was largely through her own determined efforts that she was seen by Ben Lyon, former entertainer and casting chief at Twentieth Century-Fox. He was much taken with her, arranged screen tests, changed her name (Marilyn was his suggestion, Monroe hers) and secured her a standard option contract with the studio. But Lyon's reign was almost over and, with his departure, she sank into the obscurity of a humble contract player. When Fox dropped her she had a spell at Columbia before they, too, let her go, although she did have some slightly better parts there.

The young starlet was in the wilderness when Johnny Hyde, Hollywood's most successful and influential agent, took her under his wing. Middle-aged, long-married, and suffering from a heart condition that would very soon kill him, Hyde knew that Marilyn's potential was special and was determined to see her into stardom. She had been modelling on the side to make ends meet, and had posed for the famous nude calendar pics which were to bring her so much publicity a couple of years later. Hyde fell in love with Marilyn and wanted to marry her but, to her credit, she refused. This did not deter his efforts on her behalf and, for her part, she grew not only fond of him but absolutely dependent on him for guidance, so that his death, when it came, left her profoundly shaken and raised all her old spectres of insecurity and abandonment.

Through Johnny Hyde's efforts Marilyn was cast as Louis Calhern's young mistress in Huston's *The Asphalt Jungle* for M.G.M. It was a small role but she was luminous and affecting and got herself properly noticed by the critics for the first time. The critics, in fact, were quick to spot her qualities and to enthuse over them, but M.G.M. didn't want her any more than Fox or Columbia had. Thanks to Hyde again, she followed the Huston film with one for Joseph L. Mankiewicz. In his Oscar-garlanded *All About Eve* she played Miss Caswell, introduced by George Sanders as 'a graduate of the Copacabana School of Dramatic Art'. Not much more than a cameo, the role nonetheless enhanced her reputation. Sanders later wrote in his autobiography that he absolutely knew Marilyn would achieve stardom because she so much *needed* to. Before his death Hyde persuaded a still-indifferent Zanuck to give Marilyn a six-month contract. The studio converted it to a seven-year contract when her mere presence at an exhibitors' dinner caused a sensation; they knew they were on to something but, incredibly, they didn't grasp what the something was, and continued to give her supporting roles in mediocre films.

Meanwhile, the Marilyn image was growing and her fame was spreading. The media caught on to her publicity value and, through no fault of her own, her publicity began to far outstrip her achievements. Her ingenuous witticisms (Did she have *anything* on when she posed for the nude calendar? 'Yes – the radio.') delighted both press and public; every red-blooded American male was seduced by the Monroe wiggle; the protective of both sexes wept for her deprived childhood. Her army of followers was steadily gathering conscripts and it registered at the box-office. Privately, she was working hard, she wanted to be taken seriously – a plea that would recur until her death – and she had acquired Natasha Lytess, an intellectual European of the theatre, as her dramatic coach and confidante. At the same time, she took classes at Morris Carnovsky's Actors' Lab and a little later she would attend the Russian actor Michael Chekov's school. Her serious intentions were certainly evident to herself if to nobody else and, when she later became an acolyte of Lee Strasberg and the Actors' Studio, derision was heaped upon her by a resentful Hollywood which her performance in Joshua Logan's *Bus Stop* and her union with Miller went some way to stilling.

The professional breakthrough came in 1953 with *Gentlemen Prefer Blondes*. Her funny, ingenuous gold-digger, Lorelei Lee, breathlessly delivering 'Diamonds Are A Girl's Best Friend', properly displayed her gifts for the first time, and she scored again with the less-inspired follow-up, *How To Marry A Millionaire*, leaving her co-stars Lauren Bacall and Betty Grable standing. Monroe was now a star as well as a name but wouldn't get a good role again until *The Seven-Year Itch*. She was still badly paid and had no say against poor material other than refusing to do it, which didn't endear her to studio executives. She was growing bitter and resentful, not without reason, and when astute and sensitive photographer Milton Greene suggested they set up Marilyn Monroe Productions and she go independent, she was delighted to acquiesce. The business details were labyrinthine and she was unable to avoid an obligation to make four further films for Twentieth Century-Fox within a seven-year period.

In December 1954, aged twenty-eight, Marilyn Monroe left Hollywood for New York and a new phase in her life. She lived for some time with Milton Greene and his wife Amy before taking an apartment in Manhattan. Divorced from DiMaggio, she was seeing Arthur Miller again. That they were in love was clear and during 1955 he separated from his wife. However, he was having difficulty coming to terms with the idea of divorce, particularly as he was concerned with the effects on his two children, Robert and Jane, to whom he was very attached. Consequently, most of his meetings with Marilyn were held in secret that year, and she spent much time alone, walking in Brooklyn, coming to know and love her future husband's haunts. She continued to show the same restraint that she had employed from the moment of their first meeting; she was certain that, above anything, she wanted to marry this man who, to her, represented intellectual respectability, social status and the loving and protective father she had never had and, for once in her life, self-preservation won – she knew if she pressured him in any way she would lose him.

But if Marilyn was happy to be free of Hollywood's bondage and thrilled by the promise of New York, she was also, in a little while, hopelessly adrift. She needed an anchor; a place to be and something to do, even though those pressures had driven her latterly to sleeping pills, lateness on the set and appalling tensions with her directors and fellow actors. Her shaky ego, that had come to rely on an entourage of professional aides who were also expected to act as nursemaids and confidantes, was now having to exist in isolation so that, when it was suggested to her that she meet Lee Strasberg, founder and head of the Actors' Studio, she was ready for his influence. Marilyn Monroe encountered a new perspective on acting with the Actors' Studio. They employed the Method which was Lee Strasberg's extension of the great Russian Stanislavski's technique whereby an actor is encouraged to immerse himself in the inner life of a character in order to give a truthful portrayal. To do this the actor is called upon to dig into the deepest recesses of his own emotional memory and relive his innermost feelings. It is an uncompromising, often painful and extremely self-involving process, akin to psychoanalysis and, indeed, Strasberg encouraged his students to enter analysis since he considered it helpful to their work. Lee and his wife Paula were dedicated and ruthless teachers, educated and totally absorbed in the craft and the literature of drama. Their eight-roomed apartment was lined with books from floor to ceiling; books in several languages that spilled over on to every available surface. The kitchen was a free-spirited meeting place where the disciples would gather informally to chat in an atmosphere of liberal intellectual thought and intense involvement.

This was the new world in which Marilyn Monroe found herself and, under the persuasive and encouraging guidance of Lee and Paula, she threw herself wholeheartedly into the business. She took private lessons with Lee and, in due course, joined the classes at the Actors' Studio where she always remained shy and deferential. Miller, while he came to recognize the value of Lee Strasberg's disciplines for Marilyn, had little fondness for the man and the two most important and competing strands of her existence were kept largely separate. She was not without private demons, aware that her uncertain temperament could prove a threat to her relationship with Arthur, and, anxious to bury her fears, she began seeing an analyst. But the processes of self-examination she was undergoing were viewed differently in different quarters. As Guiles explains, 'In Strasberg's view, these sessions began to liberate Marilyn. The work in the class helped her analysis, and the analysis freed her in such a way that the class took on another dimension.' But in the opinion of others who had been close to the actress for a long time, 'her preoccupation with her "emotional memory" ... triggered a disintegrating process, a fracturing of an ego that had only been reassembled with much pain a few years earlier'.

In December 1955 Strasberg decided that Marilyn was ready to perform publicly at the Actors' Studio. Terrified by the idea of exposing herself in live performance, she nonetheless prepared a scene from Eugene O'Neill's *Anna Christie*. Her approach to the project revealed to Arthur Miller the full depths of her dedication to her craft and he began to share Strasberg's perception of her talent. He now felt strongly that it would be his task to both encourage and protect his future wife in her new incarnation as a serious actress. *Anna Christie* met with a rapturous response at the Studio. Against all the odds, Monroe was becoming a Method actress and, outwardly at least, was at last enjoying a sense of self-esteem.

In 1956 Marilyn prepared to return to Hollywood to make the first of her four pictures for Twentieth Century-Fox. By now she was taking private classes with Paula Strasberg, and it was decided that Paula must accompany her. Thus was ditched, without one word either before, during or after the event, Natasha Lytess, the faithful coach who had taught Marilyn almost everything she knew. It was a pattern of behaviour that was increasingly evident in Marilyn: when she no longer needed the particular support of somebody it was as if they had never been. From now on Paula Strasberg would be the scourge of Marilyn's directors, for the star never committed anything to celluloid without her coach's approval.

On this occasion, however, filming proceeded reasonably uneventfully for a Monroe shoot. The film was *Bus Stop*, from William Inge's hit Broadway play, the director Joshua Logan, one of Broadway's finest who had worked in Moscow with Stanislavski. This, of course, was pleasing to Marilyn and, for his part, he had heard good things about her from the writer of *The Seven-Year Itch*, George Axelrod, and had been briefed by Lee Strasberg, who had told him that in his opinion Monroe was one of only two screen personalities who contained the potential for greatness; the other was Marlon Brando. Logan's initial objections to having Paula around were overcome and, in the event, the star, flexing her new Method muscles, kept pills, lateness and rows to a minimum, and delivered her finest performance to date as Cherie, the clapped out, smalltown bar-room entertainer. Although her sublime Sugar Kane in *Some Like It Hot* would come to take pride of place in the public memory, some critics still feel *Bus Stop* was Monroe's finest achievement.

Bus Stop was the last film Marilyn Monroe made while in some semblance of reasonable physical and mental health. She could not know that; she had only good things to look forward to. Arthur was finally in Reno getting his divorce and they planned to marry as soon as possible. All her dreams seemed to be coming true: she was now considered a talent to be reckoned with, she was world famous, financially solvent and, after two failed marriages that had been entered into more in a spirit of *laissez-faire* than commitment, she was about to be united with the man she had loved for ten years. If Marilyn looked forward to her marriage with eager expectancy, Miller already had twinges of foreboding. He had come to realize that, in taking on Marilyn, he was taking on half-child, half-woman, subject to violent swings of mood, needful of endless assurance and, above all, driven by an ambition that was both all-consuming and fractured by self-doubt.

But the die was cast. That he loved her was not in question, and he prepared to devote himself to the cause of saving her from herself. In May Marilyn flew back to New York where she occupied herself largely with her dog, Hugo, and her cat, who gave birth to eight kittens, while she waited for Arthur to return, a free man, from Nevada, where *he* passed the time writing a short story called 'The Misfits.' By the time he joined Marilyn in early June their relationship was common knowledge and, in a foretaste of what awaited him as Marilyn's consort, Arthur was besieged by reporters at the airport, questioning him about a wedding. One of them said, 'We only bother you about this because people want to know,' to which Miller replied, 'It is your job versus my privacy. That's a remorseless conflict.' The couple's reunion was an openly affectionate one, marred only by the coolness Arthur displayed to the Strasbergs during Marilyn's attempts to bring them together, and his suspicion of Milton Greene's business arrangements for Marilyn.

Greene had now concluded a deal for Marilyn to make *The Prince And The Showgirl* in England. The *coup* was that she would co-star with the world's most distinguished English-speaking actor, Laurence Olivier, who would also direct. Paula Strasberg was, of course, to accompany Marilyn, who naturally wanted Arthur with her too. The State Department, however, together with a Congressional sub-committee still hanging on to the remnants of McCarthyism, refused to reinstate his passport. The appalling wrangles that followed became a national, then an international, issue with respected English and American newspapers castigating the American government for its intolerable treatment of one of its most important writers. Finally, the State Department bowed to pressure, and Miller was free to travel.

Marilyn threw herself heart and soul into becoming an authentic member of the close-knit Miller family. She and her future father-in-law, Isidore, were mutually devoted almost on sight and would remain in touch when the marriage was no more. Voluntarily and enthusiastically she took instruction to convert to the Jewish faith, determined to be as close as possible to her husband in every way. By now the publicity and speculation surrounding the Monroe–Miller nuptials ensured a media circus so, to avoid this, the couple decided to marry at a moment's notice and without announcement. In the presence of a tiny handful of intimates, they were married by Judge Rabinowitz at the White Plains Courthouse on 29 June 1956. Arthur gave Marilyn a gold band inscribed 'A. to M. June 1956 Now is Forever.' The following day they married again in an official Jewish ceremony at which Lee Strasberg gave the bride away.

Shortly after the wedding Mr and Mrs Arthur Miller left for England and the filming of *The Prince And The Showgirl*. Since the journey had to serve as a honeymoon, Arthur was less than delighted to be accompanied by both Strasbergs, but he did not complain. Perhaps his worst initial experience was their departure, when they were mobbed at the airport on a scale that actually induced a sense of panic in him and wiped away all traces of the disarming, boyish grin that was one of his most attractive features. The Millers were met at London airport by Laurence Olivier and his wife, the beautiful Vivien Leigh, not to mention by the entire English press corps. Marilyn Monroe gave Britain headlines comparable to the arrival of the Duchess of Windsor, and her new husband did not escape the media either. At a press conference held at the Savoy Hotel he said of Marilyn, 'She is the most unique person I have ever met,' while she offered, 'All I can say is I've never been happier in my life.'

Laurence Olivier, an English gentleman and an artist of straightforward technical skills, had no inclination to understand either the Method or the sensitivities of its practitioners. As far as he was concerned, if there was a job to do, one simply got on and did it. He was certainly aware that Marilyn might need careful handling but he had been reassured by letters from Joshua Logan. Logan had written glowingly of Monroe's attributes, concluding that 'she's worth all the trouble'. It became clear rather soon that he had somewhat oversimplified the situation. All hell broke loose on the set of and this period really marked the beginning of the end for Marilyn, both professionally and personally.

Not much more than a week into shooting, she was in a state of anxiety and her habit of lateness was in full force. It is difficult to know what triggered her fears, but they certainly weren't helped by her lack of communication with Olivier. By halfway through the filming neither could pretend to a cordial working relationship. The rows and misunderstandings, Olivier's understandable antagonism to Paula Strasberg, his tactless handling of Marilyn, and the ever-increasing delays due to the star's non-appearance would fill a book. It is, however, worth quoting Dame Sybil Thorndike, who, when Marilyn was away ill, said, 'We need her desperately. She's the only one of us who really knows how to act in front of a camera.' Even when Marilyn kept this elderly and distinguished *doyenne* of the British theatre waiting on the set for two hours, Dame Sybil saw no reason to change her opinion.

The greater significance in all this inner disturbance of Marilyn was that it shaped her relationship with her husband in a way that doomed the marriage. Miller was sucked into Marilyn's life as a sort of buffer. He took the calls from the studio enquiring where she was; he made himself responsible for pulling her together and getting her to the set; Olivier regarded him as an ally in the battle for his wife's co-operation. For Marilyn's part, she grew increasingly dependent on Arthur, not only for love and reassurance but for day-to-day professional functions such as helping her select stills. In later years they both expressed regret that he had become so closely involved with her working life but, at the time, neither realized its extent or its damage.

Marilyn collapsed into severe instability. Guiles describes it thus: 'Her slide from partial ability to function to complete incapacity was so precipitous that Miller didn't know it was coming until it happened. Before, she had been troubled by insomnia partially relieved by pills. Now even they didn't work. As the night deepened, she became hysterical. He was unwilling to risk the amount of barbiturates that could drop her into a sodden slumber. Nightly vigils began.'

'Nightly vigils began.' This became the theme of the marriage that had begun with so much hope. Those vigils were still kept during the making of *The Misfits* when Arthur and Marilyn were barely on speaking terms. Miller had trapped himself into an unlooked-for and inappropriate role of humiliation but could not turn from the cry of need and despair which underlay his wife's behaviour. An incident occurred in England which Marilyn read as betrayal, and for which she never forgave her husband. Arthur had confided to his notebook that he was having difficulty handling Marilyn, that he felt disappointed, and that he had a modicum of sympathy for Laurence Olivier. The words are not on record but, whatever they were, Marilyn chanced on the notebook, read the entry and became hysterical. Over the years she blew up the incident and it appears as a scene in *After The Fall*, Miller's powerful semi-autobiographical play about himself and his wife.

Marilyn's New York psychiatrist was called to England and, as a

73

result of her presence and help, Paula Strasberg was despatched from the scene, Olivier and his leading lady both calmed down somewhat, and the film was completed without undue incident. Marilyn met the Queen at a royal command performance, handling the occasion impeccably, and in October the frayed Millers returned to the United States.

They lived at first in peaceful seclusion in a rented cottage on Long Island. Marilyn was still fighting insomnia but she did grow stronger and more carefree; Arthur's greatest problem was his lack of creativity. Aside from writing some excellent short stories, his energies were dissipated in taking care of his wife and his numerous drafts for new plays ended up in the fireplace. Marilyn became pregnant and joy and hope were rekindled in her life. It was an ectopic pregnancy, however, and six weeks later, in agony and with her life in danger, she was rushed to hospital for a surgical termination.

Not surprisingly after this, she became subject to severe bouts of depression, and again sought relief in large doses of Nembutal. Arthur decided to rework 'The Misfits' as a screenplay especially for Marilyn, a homage from her husband which brought her temporary cheer. One afternoon she dozed off in a chair until Arthur noticed that her breathing had become abnormally harsh and laboured. He summoned emergency medical help which saved her life but, alas, it was only the first of several near-fatal incidents. On each occasion Marilyn's crisis would be followed by several days of heightened devotion to her husband; it was almost as though she needed that dramatic a level of reassurance that he loved her. There was nothing to suggest that her overdoses were attempts at suicide – she was attempting, rather, to bury the bleakness of her fears in the oblivion of sleep.

In spring of the following year the couple bought a three-hundred-acre farm in Connecticut and there enjoyed the best period of their marriage. Arthur was hard at work on the *The Misfits*, they had close friends nearby, and Marilyn revelled in the presence of her beloved animals. This was tempered by her discovery that certain of the cattle were sent to the slaughterhouse; she was never in her life able to make the connection between meat-eating and the killing of animals, an aspect of her nature that Miller utilized for a poignant scene in *The Misfits*. Arthur built a cabin away from the house where he could work undisturbed. Marilyn, true to form, grew tired of her daily routine; her temperament required distraction, so the couple took an apartment in Manhattan, relegating the farm to a weekend retreat. She went back to classes and friendship with the Strasbergs, but her English sojourn had eroded her relationship with Milton Greene, exacerbated by Arthur's unjustifiably low opinion of Milton's business dealings. Their professional relationship was formally terminated, and Marilyn dropped the man who had had so much faith in her.

Life went on. In between bouts of hospitalization Marilyn exuded surface gaiety. She was genuinely attached to Miller's children, she enjoyed her visits to the farm, she was excited about plans for *The Misfits*. If a terrible chasm was opening up between her and Arthur, they were not acknowledging it. In August 1958 Marilyn was back in Hollywood filming *Some Like It Hot* for the great Billy Wilder. Sugar Kane would become her popular monument, but in the course of filming she seemed to lose all control and confidence. Her excesses of unreliability and nervousness on the set practically reduced Wilder to wreckage and utterly alienated her co-stars, Jack Lemmon and Tony Curtis. Nonetheless, Wilder has said of Monroe that 'A whole category of films has been lost with her gone.... The luminosity of that face! There has never been a woman with such voltage on the screen with the exception of Garbo.'

Throughout the unhappy filming Arthur played the role of Marilyn's public defender and private support. He was fast becoming a kind of emotional minion, which was hardly helpful to their relationship. They returned to New York, resuming their old routine, and proceeding with arrangements for *The Misfits*, which United Artists had agreed to finance. By the end of 1959 Miller was aware that their marriage was in a perilous state but was helpless to analyse the cause fully or to find the cure. Marilyn still depended on his presence absolutely but no longer confided in him. She recognized her own irrationalities of behaviour but was powerless to change. In February 1960 she had to make another film for Fox. Her relationship with Arthur was by now in a state of disintegration but, as Guiles expresses it, ' ... there was no question in Miller's mind of allowing her to go alone to the coast. If they could not talk together, at least he could keep her pulled enough into shape to do the film. This had become his role in her life, a guardian who slept with her and counted her pills.'

The Fox engagement contributed significantly to the destruction of Marilyn Monroe, and of her marriage. *Let's Make Love*, an inept and boring musical was the unqualified disaster of Marilyn's career. Ironically, it was also the film on which she was more reliable and co-operative than anyone could remember. The reason was not a happy one. She had fallen in love with her co-star, Yves Montand, whom she allowed to exert some control over her. A Frenchman of immense Gallic charm and sex appeal (and no mean womanizer), Montand was married to Simone Signoret, who accompanied him to Hollywood. He had played in the Paris production of Miller's *The Crucible*, and he and his wife were vociferous supporters of the political Left. The Millers and the Montands began as a congenial foursome, but in no time at all Marilyn was throwing herself at Yves with scant regard either for her husband or his wife. In due course Signoret had to leave for Europe, Miller went to Nevada to look at locations and Marilyn was free to pursue her affair with Yves. Needless to say, it ended in rejection for Marilyn, since he had no intention of leaving Simone.

The Millers had been married for four years when filming of *The Misfits* began. The making of the film was a nightmare, with factions adding to the tension. Paula Strasberg led the Marilyn camp, while director Huston attempted a neutral path but was thrown together with Miller. Gable, who had his wife with him, kept himself to himself but got on well with Marilyn who had worshipped him since childhood. It was *The Prince And The Showgirl* all over again – tormented nights and late mornings, but this time Arthur's control steadily diminished. He was publicly humiliated by his wife, who took to mocking and abusing him until, eventually, they stopped sharing a bedroom and hardly spoke to one another.

In November Marilyn Monroe announced that she and Arthur Miller had parted. A few weeks later she drove up to the farm to collect certain treasured possessions, deciding regretfully to leave her adored hound, Hugo, with Arthur. According to his account of the visit, 'It was a difficult meeting. She was obviously so lost and yet she was trying to put a face on things and make me believe that she was happy, carefree, the way she wanted to be. I think she was trying to go back to her girlhood and yet she couldn't. She was trying to surround herself with gaiety but it wasn't working.' Arthur Miller soon remarried and reverted to the style of life and work which suited him. The passion and destruction of his years with

Marilyn would be unleashed after her death – and perhaps exorcised – in *After The Fall*, a play whose intimate resonances caused huge controversy and earned him a great deal of money.

From then on Marilyn's life was a constant battle to keep the forces of darkness at bay. She was not too successful and suffered a couple of severe breakdowns. She was seeing Joe DiMaggio again and he became her mainstay in crisis as well as a loving and comforting friend. Eventually she returned to Hollywood and the final chapter of her association with Twentieth Century-Fox. She fought with the studio over material but began work on *Something's Gotta Give*, co-starring Dean Martin. On 1 June 1962, the day of her thirty-sixth birthday, Marilyn reported for work. Filming went reasonably well and she was given a birthday party on the set. It was the last day she would ever spend in a film studio. She failed to appear over the next few days and the studio fired her.

Marilyn, ill and distraught, felt utterly victimized but tried to maintain a brave façade. She was in constant touch with friends, phoning Frank Sinatra in Monte Carlo and the Strasbergs in New York. Paula came to visit briefly but had to return, although aware of Marilyn's precarious state and worried about her. By now Marilyn had a relationship with the Kennedy clan, particularly with the president's brother Robert. This connection in high places continues to fuel speculation twenty-five years after her death. The stream of articles, books and even TV documentaries suggesting that the F.B.I. was involved in her death keeps her fame alive in an atmosphere of notoriety which she didn't deserve.

During August Marilyn, who now owned a house in Brentwood, busied herself as best she could. She saw her psychiatrist daily, she saw a few friends, she played with her dog. And she took pills. In the small hours of Sunday, 4 August Marilyn Monroe was found dead of an overdose of sleeping pills. This time there had been no Arthur to rescue her. Her limp hand held a telephone receiver and it was widely believed that she was trying to phone for help when life ebbed away.

The body of Marilyn Monroe was placed in a chilled vault at the Los Angeles County Morgue where it lay waiting to be claimed. Distraught and embarrassed, none of her friends knew what to do with her until Joe DiMaggio came to the rescue. Unmistakably grief-stricken, he led the mourners at the funeral he had arranged; Lee Strasberg delivered the elegy.

Arthur Miller was not present.

TONY CURTIS

— AND —

JANET LEIGH

When handsome, dark-haired, twenty-six-year-old Bernie Schwartz from the Bronx, the son of a Hungarian-born Jewish tailor, married pretty, blonde, twenty-four-year-old Jeanette Helen Morrison from California, daughter of a Protestant insurance and real estate agent, on 4 June 1951, it was an American dream come true. These attractive young lovers were known to the world as Tony Curtis and Janet Leigh. He had just become the number one pin-up boy of the teen set in Universal's *The Prince Who Was A Thief* (1951), and she was M.G.M.'s sweetest ingenue in roles like Mrs Richard Rodgers in *Words And Music* (1948), Meg in *Little Women* and June Forsyte in *That Forsyte Woman* (both 1949). With the growing youth audience in the 1950s, it was just the romance to keep fan magazines busy for some years.

Although Tony Curtis and Janet Leigh came from vastly different backgrounds, they had much in common. Both were good-looking, up-and-coming young stars created and groomed by their respective studios and, according to one columnist, 'fearfully ambitious kids, so determined to make it ... over eager, over nice, over everything'. They were also very much in love. Yet it was a chance in a million that they would ever get together. Janet was the kind of girl Tony, brought up in the rough, tough, rundown neighbourhood of the Bronx, could only dream about. She was brought up in a comfortable home in Merced, California, wanting for nothing. At high school she was a drum majorette, wore pretty dresses, went to proms and was cover girl on the school's magazine in her freshman year. At the age of fourteen Janet eloped with a boy of eighteen, but the couple were captured a day later by her parents and the marriage was annulled. (She had lied about her age to the preacher.) Four years later she married a fellow student at the College of the Pacific, where she was majoring in music. 'Actually,' Janet admitted, 'I think every girl thinks she's going to be a housewife, and I was no exception. I never thought seriously about being a professional woman.' But when her husband's dance band didn't get any bookings, she did some fashion modelling to support them.

At the time, Janet's mother was working as a receptionist at a ski lodge in Soda Springs, California, and kept a photograph of her lovely daughter on her desk. One day, former M.G.M. star Norma Shearer, now retired and a guest at the lodge, saw the picture and was so impressed she sent it to M.G.M. who immediately signed Janet to a contract in June 1946. It was the answer to the couple's financial difficulties, although she had never done any real acting before. 'I knew I couldn't act,' Janet confessed, 'but they promised to give me dramatic lessons and the first picture I tested for was *The Romance Of Rosy Ridge* opposite Van Johnson. I'd only had a few lessons and when they told me I had the part, I said, "You can't make me do it. You promised to teach me to act."' Nevertheless, the nineteen-year-old's freshness and wholesome beauty drew a tremendous response, and stardom was soon within reach.

Young Bernie Schwartz never had it that easy. He had to shine shoes before he was ten years old to help his family. In order to survive, he joined a street gang which got into fights and went in for petty thieving. To show off, Bernie used to play a dangerous game called 'Victim', in which he would run in front of a car or truck and pretend to have been hit when they screeched to a stop. In this way he would often be given some dollars by the distressed drivers. One day his younger brother Julius was knocked down by a truck and died two days later. For many years into his adulthood Tony blamed himself for the child's death, convinced that Julius was killed emulating his elder brother whom he hero-worshipped. At seventeen Bernie joined the Navy and spent three years on war service. During that time he decided to become an actor and, when he was demobbed, took dramatic lessons and began to appear in a few productions. It was while playing the lead in Clifford Odets' boxing drama *Golden Boy*, off-Broadway in May 1949, that he was spotted by a talent scout from Universal and given a contract. Although unbilled and appearing only briefly in his first film *Criss Cross* (1949), fan mail came into the studio addressed, for example, to 'the cute fellow who danced with Yvonne de Carlo'. He then appeared under the name of Anthony Curtis in a further eight films before Tony Curtis emerged as a star in *The Prince Who Was A Thief*, a colourful Arabian Nights adventure.

In 1950, when Tony first met Janet, he was an insecure bit player and she was a composed, much-sought-after young M.G.M. star. Janet had divorced two years earlier, and was always on the arm of some eligible man. Their paths first crossed when Tony and his room-mate, a stage actor newly arrived in Hollywood called Marlon Brando, caught sight of Janet in a group at Palm Springs. Both men fancied her and managed to catch her eye, but it was Tony whose looks she preferred. Some weeks later, at a Hollywood party, he was asked by a photographer to pose with Janet, much to the chagrin of her partner. A few stilted words were exchanged between them before she returned to her escort. 'What's that guy got that I ain't?' Tony asked the cameraman. 'Janet Leigh,' he replied. 'I've got news for you,' Tony came back. 'I'm working on it.'

For two months Tony 'worked on it', but to no avail. He had little confidence and even less money. His experience of women, especially those in Janet's class, was extremely limited. He had dated Ann Blyth, with whom he had made his first screen test, for a while, and Marilyn Monroe, then a starlet at Fox. (Years later, he would have a hard time co-starring with her in *Some Like It Hot*, during the filming of which he made the remark that kissing Monroe was 'like kissing Hitler!'). But Tony met Janet again at a housewarming party given by Mel Torme and his wife. Both Tony and Janet were there with dates, although this didn't preclude Janet from asking Tony and his partner back to her house to watch TV after the party. Over coffee, Tony explained to Janet that he wanted to become a star, and that he was attempting to form an acting class. She told him she might be interested in attending herself, and asked him to call her when they began. He now felt he had a good excuse to contact her and, despite the fact that the project fell through, he plucked up the courage to telephone but not in his own voice. Cary Grant was the actor he most admired, the type of man he would have liked to be, and of whom he did an excellent imitation. In fact, it is Grant's voice he uses to seduce Marilyn Monroe in *Some Like It Hot*. Pretending to be Grant, Tony asked Janet out for a date. She accepted. 'Goodbye, my dear,' said Tony triumphantly. 'Goodbye, Tony,' she replied, rapidly replacing the receiver.

In contrast to his cocky manner, Tony was exceptionally unsure of himself in those days. 'When I first came to Hollywood,' he told his biographer Michael Munn, 'I was really like a nature boy. You never saw such a left-footed, clumsy-looking guy. I'd never been in a private home. I didn't know what it was to have a private bathroom or what forks to use.' One evening during dinner at Cole Porter's, Tony broke a beautiful champagne glass. Ethel Merman, who was sitting opposite him, said, 'Kid, don't worry about it,' and broke her own glass into pieces. Thus, Tony felt uncouth and, afraid that he might bore Janet, invited the Mel Tormes along on his first four dates with her. Finally he decided to invite her out alone, explaining that 'as dey pay me peanuts ... I can't think of a single place I could afford and which you'd approve 'cos of the big star that you are... '. Janet replied, 'It doesn't matter where we go. Whatever we do, I'm witcha!'

They were soon seeing each other twice a week, and then almost every day. Feeling relaxed in each other's company, they spent their time hiking and going to the beach. Their relationship reached a point where they felt it was time to be introduced to their respective parents. Tony insisted Janet met his folks first because he wanted to postpone meeting her mother and father for as long as possible. Helen and Manny Schwartz prepared a big meal for the couple in their small Hollywood apartment, and Manny even put on a tie for the occasion. During the meal, as father and son tucked into their roast chicken, Janet turned to Mrs Schwartz and said, 'It seems we both like to see our men eat.' The evening was a success. Manny and Helen got on well with their son's film-star girlfriend, and she adored them. Tony's visit to Janet's parents did not go down quite so well. Firstly, Tony, arriving at Mr and Mrs Morrison's large house, instead of taking the path, cut across the lawn which happened to be newly planted grass. During the evening Tony kept calling Janet's father Mr Leigh, which did not help the polite but strained conversation. Any initial reluctance on the Morrisons' part to accept Tony vanished, however, when they realized how serious Janet was becoming about him.

It was actually Universal Studios who were opposed to any thoughts of marriage between the two young stars. They wanted to protect their new investment, thinking that if Curtis married it would ruin his appeal to his growing band of teenage girl fans. He had even given his name to a hairstyle much imitated by boys at the time. When Tony visited the hairdresser, studio press agents gathered the greasy cuttings and sent them to fans. To Universal's objections to any wedding plans he might have, Tony replied, 'If my fans go to see my pictures because I'm single, then I'm in the wrong business.'

Clinging to the old proverb of 'out of sight, out of mind', Universal sent Tony on a lengthy tour of the country to promote *The Prince Who Was A Thief*, while M.G.M. sent Janet on an equally lengthy tour to stump up trade for *Angels In The Outfield*. But 'absence made the heart grow fonder'. Tony was in Chicago and Janet was in Pittsburgh, missing each other badly. It was the first time they had been separated since they had begun dating. One night Tony called her at her hotel but she was out at a party with the company. He continued to ring every ten minutes from 2 a.m. until she answered. 'I can't stand it,' he said. 'I've been so worried. Will you marry me?' Hardly hesitating, Janet replied in the positive.

On the day of their wedding Tony shook with nervousness. Janet, who had been there twice before, told him, 'It's only a wedding, darling. Brace up. It's only for the rest of our lives.' Hoping to escape the crowds – and the censure of their studios – the couple married quietly in the Marrying Room of the Pickwick Hotel in Greenwich, Connecticut on 4 June 1951. She wore a pastel-blue cotton dress, white straw hat, and white shoes and gloves. Jerry and Patti Lewis were best man and matron of honour. The few friends and relatives present then enjoyed a champagne lunch and cut into the three-tiered wedding cake baked in the shape of a castle. Afterwards they all drove to the bridal suite at the Waldorf-Astoria where they held another celebration. The studios, initially so against the marriage, now capitalized upon it to the full. Wherever the couple went they were photographed and written about. They posed obligingly at countless parties and premières, were seen feeding each other birthday cake, and relaxing at home. The Hollywood Women's Press Club presented them with the Golden Apple as the most co-operative stars. Their slightest move was detailed by the gossip columnists. Typical was this extract from *Screen Parade* in 1952: 'Tony lunches on steak and orange pop, spells badly, jitterbugs like a champion but stumbles on the tango, collects jazz records ... and numbers among his closest friends Jerry Lewis, Marlon Brando and anyone Janet thinks is nice.' A few years into the marriage they moved from their modest one-bedroomed apartment to a lavish mansion next to Pickfair in Beverly Hills. In fact, they almost seemed to have become the Pickford and Fairbanks of the 1950s.

As 'The Happiest Couple in Hollywood' lived their lives in the full glare of publicity, they had to come to terms with the realities of married life. He found it difficult to wholly give up his many years of bachelor freedom, and still hung around with 'the guys'. In spite of his fame he continued to have grave doubts about his acting career, and swallowed pills for everything from insomnia to nerves. Janet was a great believer in a well-balanced diet and regular meals, while Tony preferred to eat anything at any time. She was also extremely tidy about the house, forever cleaning up after her husband and emptying ashtrays. But adjustments were made, and after three years they were still as devoted to each other as ever. In 1953 they made *Houdini*, the first of five films in which they would co-star. *The Hollywood Reporter* commented that 'Curtis and Miss Leigh make a winning team, playing the love scenes with moving tenderness.'

Not wanting to be separated from each other for any length of time, Tony arranged for Janet to go with him to the Pacific islands where he was to film *Beachhead* (1954), before she started on *Prince Valiant* in Hollywood. Just prior to leaving with him Janet had a pregnancy test using her real name to avoid publicity. Nonetheless the press somehow got wind of it, and she was pestered on the trip by reporters wanting confirmation. When they arrived in Honolulu the couple were greeted by hundreds of fans showering them with garlands. After a few weeks Janet rang Los Angeles to find out the result of the test. On hearing that it was positive Tony and Janet were thrilled, but it was soon time for her to leave to carry out her film commitment in Hollywood. They said a fond farewell, with Tony insisting that his wife rest as much as possible.

Lonely, worried about Janet, and on location for the first time,

Tony suffered through the long, hot days filming on the island of Iloilo. He phoned her every other day to reassure himself that she was well. Although Janet always told him she was feeling fine, she was sleeping badly and suffering from nausea and depression. On the day after her twenty-sixth birthday she had a miscarriage. It was Mrs Morrison who broke the news to Tony. He immediately wrote to console his wife, but he was devastated. On his return to America he started to see a psychoanalyst. In fact, he was to spend over $30,000 on analysis in the next few years. 'Anyone who can afford to see a psychiatrist should do so.... The quicker we get rid of our problems, the better it is for the person concerned and his wife,' Tony told a reporter in 1955. 'When you live in a place like Hollywood, the strain of everything begins to tell on your mind. People who are in love suddenly find they are fighting one another. Marriages split wide open. I didn't want it happening to us.' At one particular session he managed to expunge the guilt he felt at his brother's death. He immediately phoned Janet to inform her of the breakthrough. She realized how much he needed her and determined not to allow filming to part them again. 'This marriage has got to last,' she said. 'It means a fulfilment of the real me.'

However, they were only able to make one picture together, *The Black Shield Of Falmouth* in 1954, before having a lengthy separation thousands of miles apart. Unhappy with the roles he was getting. Tony could not resist an offer from Burt Lancaster to appear opposite him in *Trapeze* to be shot in Paris under Carol Reed's direction. It was more difficult to understand why Janet accepted the female lead in *Safari*, a potboiling jungle film to be made on location in Kenya. Before her departure for Africa Janet joined her husband in Paris. Crowds witnessed Tony Curtis greeting his wife at the airport with a passionate kiss. They embraced all the way in the cab to the Hotel George V where Tony presented Janet with a diamond ring set in gold. It was a second honeymoon during which they danced every night and went hiking together daily around countryside near Paris. After a tearful parting, Tony was left in worried about Janet filming in the heart of Mau Mau country scared stiff at first,' he said at the time, 'but they tell me unit will get plenty of protection.' The making of *Safa* extremely unpleasant and uncomfortable experience everything, Janet caught a kidney infection. This w when she learnt she was pregnant again.

Despite a bad pregnancy, Kelly Curtis was born well, though prematurely, in June 1956. The baby's parents were ecstatic, and drew closer than they had ever been. Their careers, too, took new directions. Tony finally proved to the critics and himself that he was not just a pretty face with a pretty awful accent, but an actor to be reckoned with in his roles as the loathesome press agent in *Sweet Smell Of Success* in 1957, and as the racist convict in *The Defiant Ones* the following year, when Janet made *her* best film to date as Charlton Heston's threatened wife in Orson Welles' *A Touch Of Evil*. Together, in 1958, they appeared in a fluffy comedy, *The Perfect Furlough*, and in *The Vikings*, a 'Norse Opera' in which Tony rips open Welsh princess Janet's bodice so that she can row a boat more freely. On the latter film the popular couple earned a million dollars between them.

In August 1958 Tony, Janet, Dean Martin and songwriter Sammy Cahn were all in a car returning from a party at Peter Lawford's in Santa Monica when another car rammed into them. Janet, who was expecting her second child in November, became hysterical. She was unhurt but was afraid the baby might have been damaged. She was rushed to hospital where doctors confirmed that no harm had come to the unborn child. Jamie Curtis was born on schedule, a week after the death of Manny Schwartz. Heartbroken as he was, Tony kept his sorrow back for almost five months. One night, haunted by memories of his father and unable to sleep, Tony went out to the cemetery and wept at Manny's grave. 'If only you could have lived to see baby Jamie,' he cried. It was about this time that the marriage began to veer slowly and surely towards the rocks.

'We used to go to work together, come home together, go to a producer's house for dinner together, then go to bed and have five hours of sleep,' Tony explained. 'If we got five minutes alone in a closet we were lucky. It was a life – but it wasn't living life to the full. We only have one go at life and I wanted more.' No doubt the constant pressure of the press to see them as Hollywood's ideal couple contributed to the tensions. When they had tiffs, whether in private or in public, the fan magazines exaggerated them out of all proportion. Janet found solace in her two daughters, while Tony escaped by means of alcohol and drugs. Yet 1959–60 saw the release of *Some Like It Hot*, Tony's portrayal being the pinnacle of his comic art, *Operation* in which he co-starred with his idol Cary Grant, *Who*

Was That Lady?, a lively comedy featuring Curtis and Leigh together for the last time, and Alfred Hitchcock's *Psycho*, Janet's most famous role as the girl stabbed to death in the shower.

In the summer of 1961 a tragic event shattered Janet. She and the girls were on the French Riviera having a holiday for the first time without Tony when news came that her father had committed suicide. Mr Morrison had left a note blaming marital problems for his having taken an overdose. She saw it as an omen of her own marriage difficulties. The last straw came early in 1962 when Janet and the children joined Tony in Argentina and Brazil during the shooting of the Russian epic *Taras Bulba*. In the role of a Polish princess in love with dashing Cossack Curtis was seventeen-year-old German actress Christine Kaufmann. Tony, who had barely looked at another woman since Janet, was clearly smitten by the attractive, highly intelligent girl. She made the thirty-seven-year-old star feel young again, while his good looks and sensitivity appealed to her. It seemed that the romance going on in front of the cameras was being echoed away from them. In addition, Mrs Kaufmann, who had to approve everything her daughter did, actively encouraged the liaison.

Meanwhile, Janet continued outwardly to act as if nothing had happened. She told reporters, 'I'm always hearing rumours about me and Tony. But it doesn't bother me. We just ignore them. We've been married ten years and every year they come up with more stories. We're just two people and in all these years I promise you, we've had fights, but we're not going to get a divorce just because of a fight.' But everyone knew it would not be over such a fight but over a teenage actress. Janet did, in fact, have hopes of rescuing the marriage, if only for the sake of the children, but Tony saw Christine as a new beginning for him. Gossip columnists were soon blaming Christine for what looked like being the end of 'The Happiest Marriage in Hollywood'. Tony later denied this emphatically. 'It [the marriage] was falling apart and it was completely bust before I met Christine. My marriage was hopeless and people were saying you can't let it go bust. One character even said, "Where am I going for dinner if you two divorce?" When we split up it was like Jill leaving Jack.'

Actually, it was Jack leaving Jill. As soon as his work on *Taras Bulba* was over, Tony moved out of their home in Summit Drive and into a three-bedroom bungalow. A few days later Janet was found in a coma in a New York hotel room after a reputedly accidental overdose of sleeping pills, but she rallied remarkably, determined to make a new life of her own. Janet immediately filed for divorce, started dating stockbroker Robert Brandt, and threw herself into roles in the exuberant musical *Bye Bye Birdie*, in which she sang 'Put On A Happy Face', and in the appropriately titled sophisticated comedy *Wives And Lovers* (both 1963). Tony, on the other hand, coped with the break-up, which he had instigated, less well. Christine was filming in Germany and he was lonely. He spent thousands of dollars phoning her every day. He tried to see his daughters as much as possible, but they were growing away from him. While making *Forty Pounds Of Trouble* he took daughter Kelly and the young girl playing the orphan in the picture to Disneyland. However, Tony suffered guilt from what he felt was the harm he was doing to his children.

One night Tony turned up at Cary Grant's home and unburdened himself to the older man for almost three hours. 'I just talked and let out the garbage,' he said. 'Again, I needed someone to talk to. And this time I didn't want to do it to a headshrinker.'

In July 1962 Janet obtained a quick Mexican divorce. She won custody of Kelly and Jamie as well as a Rolls-Royce, a Cadillac, half their cash, stocks, bonds, cattle and oil properties, plus one dollar a year token alimony. Janet saved Tony the annual dollar by marrying Brandt two months later. Tony had to wait until Christine turned eighteen before they could marry in February 1963. It was a five-minute ceremony held in Los Angeles with Kirk Douglas and his wife acting as best man and matron of honour. The bride was four months pregnant.

Tony's marriage to Christine Kaufmann lasted four years, and was followed by an eleven-year marriage to English model Lesley Allen. He also had several much-publicized affairs, including those with Soraya Kashoggi, the estranged wife of a Saudi Arabian multimillionaire, and with twenty-one-year-old actress and dancer Andria Savio, who helped him get over his drug problem. However, he would always look back with nostalgia to his first marriage. Although he had two daughters by Christine and two sons by Lesley, Tony often regretted the rupture that took place between himself and his eldest daughters. After the divorce, he realized, his kids began to treat him as a happy-go-lucky uncle. In

1970 Janet explained, 'For me love and marriage were coupled with a need for a stable existence. I've never underestimated love, it's a very powerful emotion. With Tony...we lasted ten years together, and that's quite a time. Particularly in this business. When we broke up I told the kids, "Mummy and Daddy still love you, but maybe their own love just grew in different directions".'

Until recently, Jamie Lee Curtis, now a star in her own right, would not speak to her father. Her success in films like *Halloween* and *The Fog*, in which she co-starred with her mother, made Tony very proud of his daughter, but 'she has not forgiven me for the old me. In not forgiving me, she is not forgiving herself.' Gradually, both Jamie Lee and Janet have been reconciled with Tony. Jamie Lee Curtis, who has her mother's looks and her father's name, and much of his character, is the living reminder of *the* Hollywood love story of the 1950s.

RITA HAYWORTH
— AND —
ORSON WELLES

n the late 1940s Rita Hayworth, the first Hollywood sex
symbol to be officially labelled 'the Love Goddess', was
Columbia's most valuable box-office asset. Yet in 1946
Orson Welles, the *enfant terrible* of the film industry,
managed to desecrate her image in the eyes of the American
nation in one of his minor masterpieces, *The Lady From Shanghai*.

The film, written and directed by Welles and co-starring himself and Rita Hayworth, was a box-office disaster. A brooding,
baroque, sometimes incoherent thriller, with a typically dark
Wellesian comment beneath its surface on the corruption of
wealth, was received with apoplectic disfavour by Harry Cohn,
the notoriously ruthless and autocratic mogul in charge of
Columbia. So violent was his dislike that the film's release was
delayed until 1948. In spite of its adverse reception by critics and
public alike, however, it has since been reappraised and now
occupies a prime position in any retrospective of the films of
Orson Welles.

However, it was less the subject-matter that upset Harry Cohn
than the treatment of the film's leading lady, Rita Hayworth,
otherwise Mrs Orson Welles. An enchanting dancer and an excellent actress, she was one of the outstanding beauties of her time.
The camera loved her as only a camera can, and ignited a vibrant
on-screen sensuality that made her the object of men's desires
wherever in the world her films were shown. She was, in short, a
Big Star. Her crowning glory and her most famous physical
feature was her rich, flowing, auburn hair, the envy of all women
who aspired to beauty. As The Lady of her latest film's title,
however, Miss Hayworth was unveiled to the world shorn of her

tresses and with what little remained dyed blond. It was a shock to the American nation, and a tribute to the star's unquestioning faith in her director.

But by the time of which we speak Rita Hayworth and Orson Welles were nearing the final curtain in their personal sad play about love magically found only to be irretrievably lost. When the couple met at a supper party given by the actor Joseph Cotten and his wife in the summer of 1943, Welles was twenty-eight years old and Hayworth a year younger. Each had experienced one marriage that had ended in divorce, both were uniquely attractive, and they shared the condition of international fame which left them constantly exposed to the glare of publicity and gossip. So much for common ground.

Rita was a deeply shy and retiring woman, unsure of herself, warm-hearted and sympathetic. She was very rich but simple in her tastes and aspirations, and extremely well liked by the denizens of the film jungle. Orson was an extrovert, demanding, professionally wayward and privately promiscuous egomaniac. Flamboyant and charismatic, he was a brilliant artistic rebel and liberal political orator with a taste for extravagant self-indulgence. He was also as good as penniless, since he had a cavalier disregard for money, looking upon it only as a necessary evil to finance his projects, and his large earnings were continuously absorbed by the debts he incurred to colleagues, backers and his ex-wife. His attitude was that of an irresponsible and impractical gambler playing the tables recklessly with somebody else's funds, and without any regard to the consequences. It was a ruinous condition that would attend him all his life, and which had already earned him the general opprobrium of those who ran and financed the big business known as the film industry.

Writer, actor, designer, broadcaster, director and producer, Orson Welles was once aptly labelled a 'genius without portfolio'. He would become a citizen of the world, but he was born in Kenosha, Wisconsin in 1915 and raised in comfortable, middle-class circumstances by a rumbustious, hard-living inventor father and, until her death when Orson was only eight, a cultivated, artistic mother. The boy Orson exhibited signs of an exceptional mind and imagination early on, and was eventually sent to the Todd School at Woodstock, Illinois. This was a stylish establishment, run along liberal and progressive lines designed to nurture the individuality of the students. There, encouraged by the theatre-loving head-master, Roger Hill, who became his life-long friend, young Welles drew, painted, staged magic shows, and performed in plays and musicals, all of which demonstrated his prodigious gifts.

At sixteen, spurning the idea of going to college, Welles made his way to Ireland. With his enormous physique, an unruly style of dress that would have been appropriate to the Sixties rather than the early Thirties, and an exquisitely resonant speaking voice, he seemed older than his years. With breathtaking confidence he talked his way into the prestigious Gate Theatre in Dublin and spent a season acting and designing under the expert eyes of Hilton Edwards and Michael MacLiammoir who ran the company.

On his return to the States, Welles found himself without employment and spent time with Roger Hill at Woodstock, work-ing with him on compiling new acting editions of Shakespeare's plays for publication. He grew bored and restless and left for Morocco and Spain, where he wandered until his money ran out. Home again, a chain of fortunate meetings led to an engagement touring the country as an actor with the famous company run by Guthrie McClintick and his wife, the actress Katherine Cornell. In the summer of 1934, during an interval before the company's New York season was to open, Welles decided to stage a festival of plays at Woodstock, and to invite Edwards and MacLiammoir to come from Ireland as the guest stars. It was a measure of his persuasive powers that these distinguished actors accepted. Helped by Roger Hill's connections, the season was not only financed but was publicized to the hilt, and a visit to Woodstock became one of the summer's fashionable events. The mastermind behind it all was a mere nineteen years old.

It was at the festival that Welles met an attractive young socialite and aspiring actress named Virginia Nicholson. Accord-ing to Welles' biographer, Charles Higham, 'Welles was attracted to her instantly. So far as is known, he had not had a romantic interest in women before; his preoccupation with his career and his extreme egomania had rendered him more or less oblivious to women as serious sexual objects or even as human beings. But there was something about Virginia that fascinated him. . . . ' The consequence of this youthful passion was that, at a candlelit ceremony held in the afternoon of 23 December 1934, Miss Nicholson became the first Mrs Orson Welles.

The couple went to New York where Orson began to pursue his career with the awesome energy and manic drive that were his professional hallmarks. His rise to eminence was meteoric. By the age of twenty-two, when he co-founded the Mercury Theatre Company with John Houseman, he had already directed his now legendary experimental, all-black production of *Macbeth*, and was an established star of stage and radio. Radio was a very powerful medium before the age of television and, in 1938, Orson capitalized on his position as a broadcaster to put out his notorious 'War of the Worlds' programme. The announcement, masquerading as fact, that the Martians had landed and the destruction of America was imminent was so successful a hoax as to unleash panic across the country, and the authorities had to step in to restore calm. The broadcasting company understandably failed to appreciate his efforts, but he became a household name.

Also in 1938, Virginia gave birth to a daughter, somewhat perversely named Christopher, but the marriage was not happy. Orson was seldom to be found at home, and his interest in his wife and child was minimal compared to his obsessional absorption with his work. He had also developed a taste for attractive women which he indulged without restraint – a state of affairs of which Virginia became all too unhappily aware. By February 1940 the couple were divorced and Welles had arrived in Hollywood at the request of George Schaefer, head of production at R.K.O. studios, to start work on his first feature film. History has come to judge that film as the undisputed testament to his genius – *Citizen Kane*.

By the time Orson Welles met Rita Hayworth, *Citizen Kane* had come and gone, having caused a furore and unleashed the full wrath of William Randolph Hearst, the newspaper magnate, who saw the film as a vicious portrait of himself. His columnists had waged war on Welles and R.K.O and the film had failed to make money. Welles had also completed the stylish, gothic drama *The Magnificent Ambersons*, which had led to violent rows with the studio over its editing, and an unsuccessful film called *Journey Into Fear*. The balance of his output consisted of a vault full of footage for a film called *It's All True* shot during many months of fraught location in South America and never completed. Costs escalated so wildly that the R.K.O. executives pulled the plug on the project, thereby almost completely cooking the director's goose with the major Hollywood studios. Thus, by the summer of 1943, Welles was a film-maker in search of a film. On the personal front, he was footloose and fancy-free, having ended a long and passionate affair with the Mexican beauty Dolores Del Rio, and a short and passionate affair with the exquisite black singer Lena Horne.

Rita Hayworth's life to this point had followed a very different path from that of the man with whom destiny would unite her. She was the first child (two brothers followed) of Eduardo Cansino and his wife Volga. He was a Spanish dancer of some note and accomplishment who had been brought to America where he and his sister, billed as The Dancing Cansinos, enjoyed a high level of Broadway success.

Eduardo's daughter, Margarita Carmen Cansino, was taught to dance at the age of four and, by the time she was seven, had joined the family vaudeville act. She was a shy, reserved child, raised lovingly but strictly, who was taught the modesty, manners and morals befitting a respectable Roman Catholic Spanish girl. She was also imbued with a sense of loyalty to her family and professionalism in her craft that found expression in an intense and dedicated desire to please those who loved her and had expectations of her. When, after a sheltered, chaperoned girlhood, she found herself adrift in Hollywood, the strands of loyalty and discipline in her character transferred themselves to her lovers, husbands, and to the all-powerful Harry Cohn who exercised a despotic control over her career.

In the 1920s the Cansinos moved to Hollywood where, until a combination of the Depression and the public's diminished enthusiasm for screen musicals deprived him of both funds and work, Eduardo did well as a coach and choreographer, also dancing in a few films. In 1931 Margarita stepped in at the last minute to replace her cousin's injured partner in a live dance prologue at the première of the film *Back Street*. From the audience Eduardo saw his daughter with new eyes and hit upon a solution to supporting his family through the prevailing hard times: he would start a new dancing duo with Margarita as his partner. However, under the liquor laws, the girl's age precluded employment in American nighclubs, so the family crossed the border into Mexico where no such restrictions were in force.

Agua Caliente, near Tijuana, was a fashionable hangout for moneyed Americans who came to enjoy themselves at the golf course and the race-track by day, at the casino and the glitzy, raffish clubs by night. It was there that thirty-six-year-old Eduardo Cansino and his fourteen-year-old daughter – taken to be a husband and wife team or, at the very least, a brother and sister act – found themselves performing with a good measure of success to audiences who included talent spotters, columnists, producers and directors from Hollywood. Margarita, ever obedient to her parents' wishes, would spend the breaks between shows locked in the dressing-room, away from the questionable influences of the sophistication that surrounded her, and filled her time reading the movie magazines which so fascinated and intrigued her. She accepted her lonely lot without complaint, but develped a growing awareness of feeling suffocated by her enclosed environment. If only she could work with new and different people, be shown new and different avenues to explore....

Margarita's nervousness, therefore, was tempered with excited anticipation when her opportunity came. She was spotted dancing by Winfield Sheehan, production head at Fox Studios, and taken – with her father's agreement, of course – to Hollywood for screen tests, before being signed to a standard renewable six-month contract. The shy but ambitious teenager who, in those days, was reminiscent of a young, cut-price Dolores Del Rio or Lupe Velez (the Mexican look was fashionable in films at the time), worked inordinately hard. She embraced with fervour the obligatory classes in how to talk, how to walk, how to act; she learned to swim, to ride, to play tennis; she went on a strict diet to enhance her already lovely figure; and she acquired the art of patience in posing endlessly for publicity stills. What she didn't do was have fun. When not at work she lived quietly at home under the supervision of her parents, who had come with her.

The rewards for her efforts were few. With her name now shortened to Rita, Miss Cansino danced her way, unnoticed, through a clutch of forgettable musicals before progressing to tiny roles, where she spoke as well as danced, in a string of forgotten B-pictures. Then, in 1935, Fox merged with Twentieth Century. Darryl F. Zanuck was now the boss, and Rita's mentor, Winfield Sheehan, found himself out in the cold. Zanuck had Rita groomed for a starring role and she gave her all to the preparation for the tests. In the end she not only did not make the tests, Darryl Zanuck decided not to renew her contract. The

Cansino family's dreams of glory were temporarily shattered.

Meanwhile, at Fox Rita had met a man named Edward Judson who was visiting the lot where she was filming. Something of a mystery figure, Judson was an opportunist with a clever eye to the main chance, and a talent for making the most of his 'connections'. He had spotted Rita's potential and persuaded Eduardo, in the dark days of his daughter's disappointment, to consign her to his professional guidance. Under Judson's careful instruction the Rita Hayworth image was born. He chose her clothes and her jewels, he escorted her to the fashionable nightspots which were the essential haunts of stars and would-be stars, he taught her how to conduct herself, and controlled her every move. His masterstroke was to have her hairline raised by electrolysis and the hair itself dyed red.

Edward Judson talked an indifferent Harry Cohn into giving his protegée a contract at Columbia, in those days a minor studio. The cycle of B-pictures, familiar to Rita from her Fox days, continued and, in 1937, she married Judson who, more than twenty years her senior, had adroitly replaced Eduardo as her father figure. Finally, a professional break came with a supporting role in *Only Angels Have Wings*. It was released in 1941 and Rita, now renamed Hayworth, made an impression – if not on Harry Cohn – over at Warner Bros., who hired her from Columbia for *Affectionately Yours*, and a co-starring role opposite James Cagney in *The Strawberry Blonde*, both released in 1941. That was, in fact, quite a year for Rita Hayworth. The same Darryl Zanuck who had fired her now paid a substantial amount of money to Harry Cohn to borrow her for the role of the temptress who seduces Tyrone Power in *Blood And Sand*. She gave an excellent performance and looked ravishing in Technicolor. Back at Columbia she was magically teamed with Fred Astaire in *You'll Never Get Rich*. Harry Cohn was beginning to see the light, and had her advertised as 'The Most Exciting Girl On The Screen.'

By the end of 1941 Margarita Carmen Cansino was, as Rita Hayworth, a major star – the biggest Columbia had ever owned – and Hollywood's most potent Love Goddess. She was also separated from Judson who, having achieved his purpose in promoting Rita's career, had little to offer as a husband. Rita's mother had always disliked and mistrusted him, and he didn't get on particularly well with Eduardo. It was also clear that he regarded Rita as a commodity from which he deserved to profit (an attitude with which she loyally agreed) and in 1942 they were divorced, with Judson extracting every penny he could from his former wife by way of receiving his dues.

For the first time in her still young life Rita Hayworth was free to enjoy herself. She was finally liberated from the shackles in which first her father and then her husband had bound her. By the time her divorce was finalized she was in the throes of a passionate romance with Victor Mature, her co-star on *My Gal Sal*, a musical which she was making for Fox where Mature was a contract star. Victor Mature was virile, outgoing and fun to be with, and it was hardly surprising that Rita found the interlude highly enjoyable. It wasn't all plain sailing though. Rita, the darling of the press, came in for her first taste of their disapproval because, for reasons that were not entirely clear, they disliked her beau. Their public disfavour fanned the flames of Harry Cohn's ire, but it seems likely that his 40-carat star quite enjoyed defying him since, when Victor went east to do service with the coastguard, she disobeyed her boss's orders by going to visit him. She returned from Connecticut sporting a ring that Victor had given her but denying all rumours of an engagement.

It is a matter of record that Victor Mature was very much in love with Rita Hayworth and would have liked to marry her. For her part, she tasted the heady delights of infatuation for the first time, and was certainly fond of her desirable escort, but true love for a man was not an emotion that Rita had yet experienced. Then, one evening, with Mature three thousand miles away, Rita accepted that dinner date at the Cottens' house where one of the guests was Joseph Cotten's good friend and colleague Orson Welles. The attraction between Orson and Rita was instant. According to Miss Hayworth's biographer John Kobal, 'When the right man presented himself, Rita had no trouble deciding, though the columnists, led by a vitriolic Louella Parsons, disliked him even more than Mature.... Rita was as impressed and dazzled as everyone else had been by the genius who conceived ... *Citizen Kane*.' And in Edward Epstein and Joseph Morella's life of Rita Hayworth, the authors note that the couple 'overwhelmed each other during the courtship. Orson's many interests impressed and fascinated Rita. He let her be herself....

He was a dazzling fountain of ideas, a three-ring circus performing just for her.'

When, therefore, Orson invited Rita to dine with him the following evening, she accepted with alacrity. From Orson's point of view, to quote Charles Higham, 'In a city filled with beautiful women, Rita was among the most beautiful, an authentic goddess possessed of an especially sweet, shy, gentle nature and an intelligence that was often ignored because she was so attractive and lacked self-confidence.' Not that Orson, as we have already remarked, was any stranger to beautiful women but, as Higham has observed, Rita was different in that ' ... she represented no threat to a colossal ego such as Welles'. In every way, he felt, she was perfect for him; not only was she devastatingly pretty, she was not at all challenging or brassy – as so many Hollywood women were.... '

It wasn't long before the couple were seen together constantly, although they tried to frequent only the most discreet and quiet places. The columnists had a field day concocting gossip about 'Beauty and The Brain', as they were somewhat snidely dubbed, and Louella Parsons surpassed herself with a public article begging Rita to free herself from Orson's clutches. Harry Cohn's fury at the affair was immense, but he was powerless to stop the relationship. Rita joined Joseph Cotten and Agnes Moorehead in Orson's magic show where she was nightly sawn in half by her lover. By day, she reported to the studio as usual, working on *Cover Girl* with Gene Kelly – one of her biggest hits as it turned out, and one of her most lastingly famous films. She was ecstatically happy in a way that she had never even dreamed existed – she was utterly, completely and contentedly in love for the first time in her life and, although she would later find fleeting echoes of this fulfilment with Prince Aly Khan, she would never again know real love in so enriching a fashion.

Orson Welles, too, displayed an evident devotion to Rita that augured well for both of them. While he was entranced with her beauty and captivated by the warmth of her personality, he also admired and respected her as an actress. He didn't patronize her for her lack of education; rather, he encouraged her to develop her mind and her knowledge. He drew up reading lists for her in literature, politics, philosophy; he guided her to an appreciation of art and music; he took her seriously as a human being while cherishing her as a woman. Rita responded to his efforts with total commitment and characteristic devotion, determined to live up to the standards he set for her, and for himself. Their love blossomed and on 7 September 1943 they were married.

The wedding took place, with no advance publicity, during Rita's lunch-break from the day's filming of *Cover Girl*. They exchanged their vows at the Santa Monica Superior Court, kissed lovingly, and Mrs Orson Welles returned to Columbia Studios for the afternoon session. Perhaps the day's most poetic touch was that, during that afternoon, Rita, at her most ravishingly lovely, filmed the wonderful 'white wedding' scene for the film. That night she was back on stage being sawn in half by her husband for the magic show.

Until *Cover Girl* finished shooting the newlyweds, who were living in Orson's modest rented house, saw little of each other. When filming was over, they settled down to enjoy married life in which their chief occupations were to give intimate dinner parties for friends and to dine alone in out-of-the-way Mexican restaurants. A special pleasure for both of them consisted in taking spontaneous trips across the border to Mexico itself, where they abandoned themselves to carefree, sometimes even irresponsible, fun, revelling in both the atmosphere and each other's company. In contrast to the strains and rifts with her parents that were caused by her first husband, Rita was now able to bask in the joy of a united family. Her new husband enjoyed the company of her parents, and liked her adored grandfather. Indeed, he took special delight in listening to Rita converse with the old man in Spanish. He delighted, too, in her femininity, her serenity and even her nervousness. He was both attentive and protective, and she worshipped her extraordinary husband. All in all, the early days of their marriage confounded the Cassandras who had predicted disaster.

After the release of *Cover Girl* the couple took a trip to New York where Orson had various projects to pursue, including his political campaigning on behalf of President Roosevelt. Rita looked forward to enjoying a feast of live theatre. The visit was intended as a belated honeymoon but, in reality, Rita had become such a celebrity that she could barely leave the hotel for fear of being mauled by the over-enthusiastic crowds that collected wherever she went. It was with some relief, therefore, that they returned to Hollywood, and the new, rather more luxurious home, complete with pool, that they had recently acquired. When Rita reported back for work in May she was two months pregnant. Harry Cohn, predictably, had hysterics; his star was radiant.

The new film, *Tonight And Every Night*, was set in wartime London. It required a long and gruelling schedule, and called for some demanding dance routines from Rita who, through a combination of pregnancy and the influence of her husband's gargantuan appetite, had put on a lot of weight. She more than survived the ordeal, however, and it was all over by 17 December 1944 when she gave birth to her first baby, a girl whom they named Rebecca. The Cansinos joined their daughter, grand-daughter and son-in-law for a family Christmas. On the face of it, life couldn't have been better and, indeed, Rita's love for Orson was stronger than ever. She doted upon him.

But the couple's happiness was not destined to last. Rita's nature required, more than anything else, a settled domestic family life. Orson was the exact opposite – a restless spirit whose energies drove him to be always on the move, physically and mentally. Furthermore, he was not properly engaged in work, which frustrated him, and, much as he adored his lovely wife, he was beginning to find it very irksome to be seen merely as her escort and relegated to fodder for the social and gossip columns of Hollywood. It was no fault of Rita's, but it was understandable that, to a man of Orson's giant intellect and creativity, this could not have been a satisfactory state of affairs. He had come the closest that he ever would to being a devoted husband, and even made efforts to be a loving father but, as a friend summed it up, 'He viewed Rebecca as an exquisite toy, but his thoughts were always on some project or other.'

For some months Rita had tried to accustom herself to her home being overrun with associates of Orson – colleagues, business advisers, secretaries. He conducted frenetic conferences at all hours of the day and night. To someone of Rita's nature it was like a madhouse from which she felt alienated and, although these disturbances in no way diminished her love for him, she constantly tried to get him to change his ways. This, of course, was a hopeless task, since it was anathema to a man of Orson's temperament and habits to consider any limitations on his freedom. After the family Christmas of 1944 Orson left for the east coast to continue with his political engagements and to write a syndicated column.

And so began the slow, sad, drifting apart of two exceptional people whose love for each other was never in any doubt but who couldn't live with the conditions necessary to its survival.

The year 1945 got off to a very painful start for Rita. Her mother, to whom she was deeply attached, died suddenly of a burst appendix at the tragically early age of forty-five. The loss was devastating to Rita and her grief and loneliness were to haunt her for some time to come. She told Orson not to interrupt his work in New York and he took her at her word, later admitting that it was probably a serious misjudgement on his part. She obviously needed his presence and was hurt by his absence. Revealingly, he commented that, 'I dare say that's another instance in which a woman said the opposite of what she meant.'

When Orson did return home discord began to make itself felt and the couple even had words in public at a nightclub, sparked off by the appearance there of Victor Mature. At home, distance grew, with separate bedrooms becoming more or less the order of the day, ostensibly because of the very different hours they were keeping. Professionally, Orson at long last got a film offer when Sam Spiegel asked him to star in *The Stranger*, about an ex-Nazi war criminal in hiding in America. Welles wanted to direct the film as well as act in it and, after many months of persuasion, coercion and negotiation, Spiegel gave in. Involvement with this undertaking, plus his usual juggling with a dozen other projects simultaneously and his continuing journalistic work, kept Welles more than fully occupied.

Rita, meanwhile, began work on the film that was to provide her most enduring image: *Gilda*. This erotic *film noir* in which, clad in a slinky black strapless gown by Jean Louis, she provocatively sang 'Put The Blame On Mame' to a hypnotized Glenn Ford, took the world by storm and remains a monument to Hayworth's beauty and sensuality. She and co-star Ford conveyed a powerful chemistry which existed off screen, too, but only tacitly. By the end of the year, with her husband away again, Rita reluctantly announced a marital separation and began dating Tony Martin, the popular singer who had been recently divorced from Fox blonde Alice Faye. A whirlwind affair with Martin ended as suddenly as it had begun when Rita and Orson reunited. Thus began a series of reconciliations and partings that would drag on and on. Clearly, and by all accounts, neither wanted the marriage to end. Rita, particularly, was very much in love with her husband and would spend the next year or two alternating between hope and despair.

In 1946 Welles embarked on an extremely ambitious, large-scale Broadway venture – a musical adaptation of Jules Verne's *Around the World in 80 Days*. His co-producer was the flamboyant showman Mike Todd who would later gain Hollywood immortality with his screen version, but his initial effort resulted in failure. Costs escalated on what was a wildly expensive extravaganza and, with opening night not far off, the money ran out. In desperation Welles called the one man he could think of who would be good for an immediate fifty thousand dollars – Harry Cohn. Much as Cohn disliked Orson, he was a gambler by nature and agreed to invest the cash. In return Orson agreed that, in the event of Harry failing to get his money back, he would make a film for Columbia.

And so *The Lady From Shanghai* came into being. By now the Welles marriage appeared to be well and truly over. Rita was escorted by a string of eligible Hollywood bachelors and Orson was having an affair with actress Barbara Laage. But their strength of feeling for each other was not dead and, loyal and loving as ever, Rita agreed to star in her husband's film. It seemed that once more there were hopes of a reconciliation. The location filming, much of it aboard Errol Flynn's luxury yacht, was fraught with difficulties, not least among them Rita being taken ill and collapsing with a high temperature. She recovered, of course, but it was some time before she was really well.

The Lady From Shanghai marked Orson Welles' farewell to Hollywood for many years. (He would only direct one more American film, *Touch Of Evil*, a decade later.) He went to Europe to embark on the next phase of his bizarre and brilliant career and, *en route*, became infatuated with the Italian actress Lea Padovani. She couldn't cope with his temperamental excesses and the affair ended, but not before Rita, still hoping that she could save her marriage, heard about it. In 1947 *Down To Earth*, in which Rita appropriately played a goddess, was released to general acclaim and in November of that year she started filming

– again co-starring with Glenn Ford – a much less successful film, *The Loves Of Carmen*. It was Rita Hayworth's last film appearance for four years.

By now divorce proceedings against Orson Welles were under way (the divorce would not be final until late 1948). This time there was no going back, although the couple would meet in Europe and give rise to speculation that they were together again. Rita's comments on the failure of the marriage were largely confined, without apparent bitterness, to remarks such as, 'You can't live twenty-four hours out of twenty-four with a genius.' Welles showed restraint with sentiments such as, 'Rita is a nice, lovely, unspoiled and natural girl. I still admire her tremendously.' Under these façades lurked a sense of loss that would not leave either of them. To quote Charles Higham again, 'Rita ... was as far removed from Orson as anyone could be; yet his attraction to her beauty and her attraction to his forcefulness and intellect drove them into a relationship to which neither was properly attuned.' And – we might add – which drove them apart finally.

In the spring of 1948 Rita Hayworth sailed for Europe. Lonely, heartbroken and unwell, she concluded her tour in the South of France where she hoped to recuperate. Cannes was the glamorous playground of the fabulously wealthy, the idle, pleasure-seeking, international set whose ranks were graced with assorted royalty. Impervious to the delights that beckoned, Miss Hayworth rested in quiet seclusion, resisting the endless invitations from powerful and attractive men, including no less a personage than the Shah of Persia. Eventually, however, Elsa Maxwell, the world's most renowned, influential and persuasive society hostess, lured the reluctant star to a supper party.

Rita made a late and dazzling entrance. She was at her most breathtaking – Gilda made flesh and blood – and the assembled company was suitably entranced. Nobody there, however, was quite as captivated as the heir to the Ismaili Islamic empire, Prince Aly Khan. Aly Khan was – and in modern legend remains – the twentieth century's most accomplished playboy and its most irresistible womanizer. He was English-educated, exceptionally charming and attractive, and in line to inherit a fortune; beautiful women were the playthings of which he never tired, and he collected them in awesome numbers. Separated from his wife, Aly was free to do as he pleased. The prince, who happened to be a film buff, took one look at 'Gilda' and Rita Hayworth's fate was sealed.

Prince Aly Khan laid siege to Rita Hayworth. Their courtship was conducted in the glare of unparalleled and often tasteless publicity. The world's press, like a pack of predatory beasts, hounded the couple across Europe, which they traversed in a vain quest for peace and privacy. Their romance was the stuff of which other people's dreams are made: a modern Don Juan relentlessly wooing and pursuing a fabled beauty amidst surroundings of glittering opulence. Finally Rita, in an attempt to bury her past with Orson, could no longer resist the blandishments of Aly's charm and the promise of his protection.

On Friday, 27 May 1949, under a perfect azure sky from which the sun shone brilliantly, the shy, introverted daughter of a Spanish dancer who had been catapulted into screen stardom through the efforts of her first husband became, in marrying her third, Hollywood's first royal princess. The wedding took place in the town hall at Vallauris, a pretty village nestling in the foothills above Cannes. The mayor declared a public holiday; the roads were jammed with crowds eager to catch a glimpse of the couple; their vows were exchanged in the presence of the world's press. A lavish reception followed at the prince's sumptuous villa. It was an occasion to rival any tale in the *Arabian Nights* and to far outstrip the excesses of any Hollywood extravaganza.

The differences in background, morals, lifestyle and culture between Rita and her prince were so extreme as to doom them to failure from the outset. The marriage was passionate, stormy and unhappy, and Rita grew to know a loneliness and isolation far beyond anything she had experienced with Orson Welles. The couple had a daughter, the Princess Yasmin, and finally, in 1951, Rita literally fled from Aly, taking her little daughter with her, and returned to Hollywood.

Sick at heart, Rita Hayworth tried to pick up the threads of her former life. She had sought solace from her grief over Orson in the arms of another larger-than-life man and had only loneliness to show for it. Harry Cohn, who had never forgiven her departure, vented the full force of his sadism on Rita, reducing her to pleading for work which, when he condescended to give it to her, was inferior. Ruthlessly, he had groomed a new star to take Rita's place – Kim Novak.

The story of Rita Hayworth and Orson Welles has a sad – indeed, in Rita's case, a tragic – ending. Welles lived out his life largely in Europe, pursuing ever more fantastical projects, the most ambitious of which he never completed. He married again, the Countess Paola Mori Di Girfalco, with whom he found a modicum of calm happiness, largely, one has to conclude, because Paola was prepared to accommodate his passions for other women. To the end of his life, however, it was said that wherever he journeyed he would haunt any nightclub where a performer had some vague resemblance to Rita Hayworth. Clearly, this giant among men took the fragile memory of his red-headed goddess with him to the grave. He died in 1985 at the age of seventy.

As for Rita Hayworth, whose fame and beauty had been such that her picture was painted on the atomic bomb dropped at Bikini (a questionable tribute that appalled her), her life went from bad to worse. She became involved with crooner Dick Haymes, a somewhat unsavoury character of questionable principles and unpleasant temper, and married him. The alliance brought her nothing but misery, and she divorced him within two years. The Love Goddess's career was sliding. She was no longer on a fat contract at Columbia and she began to lean rather too heavily on alcohol.

Matters seemed to improve when she was asked to co-star with Burt Lancaster in the film version of Terence Rattigan's successful play *Separate Tables*, a prestige production which won an Oscar for David Niven. The producer who cast her was James Hill, a forty-year-old bachelor who, inevitably, fell for Rita and whom she married, more in a spirit of clutching at the straws of security than as a result of passion. Their domestic relationship dragged on for three years during which time Rita's drinking became very heavy indeed. In 1960 it fell to Hill to break the news that Aly Khan, aged forty-nine, had been killed at the wheel of his Lancia. His companion was the French model Bettina, whom he had intended to marry. Rita, desperately upset at the news, had to break it to Yasmin. It was an ugly shock that only added to her weakening condition. Her divorce from Hill saw the end of her fifth and final attempt at happiness.

By the mid-1970s she was certifiably an alcoholic. There were still public appearances, and even one or two successful professional engagements, such as the film of *Pal Joey* with Frank Sinatra and Kim Novak, but her behaviour was becoming increasingly unstable and it was clear that she was not at all well. In the winter of 1977 Rita collapsed while attending an art exhibition and was rushed to hospital. The doctor in whose care she was placed issued a statement to the effect that she was 'gravely disabled as a result of mental disorder or impairment by chronic alcoholism'. The former star was finally out of control and Yasmin arranged for her to be admitted to Silver Hill, the exclusive clinic for disturbed patients. Her sojourn there seemed to do the trick. She stopped drinking and once again looked good, but it was not long before her behaviour indicated that something was seriously wrong.

In 1981 it was publicly announced that Rita Hayworth was suffering from Alzheimer's Disease. Clearly, her drinking had been a red herring: in fact she was the tragic victim of this vicious form of mental ailment, which begins by affecting the memory and can end in total, childlike senility of which there is no known cause and for which there is no cure.

At the time of writing Rita Hayworth is still alive. She is in the legal guardianship of her daughter Yasmin, and is in the constant care of nurses. The beautiful woman who once, with great sadness, said, 'Every man I've known has fallen in love with Gilda and wakened with me,' is no more. She is a celluloid legend, whose only tangible proof of her love for Orson Welles is rolled up in a tin can labelled *The Lady From Shanghai*.

PAUL NEWMAN
— AND —
JOANNE WOODWARD

I n 1971, after thirteen years of marriage and nineteen years of friendship with Joanne Woodward, Paul Newman, giving one of his rare interviews, said, 'For two people with almost nothing in common we have an uncommonly good marriage.' His wife, at the same period, proffered the observation that, 'Certainly we're different. That's what keeps a marriage alive, plus the fact that I adore him. Just that.'

This 'uncommonly good marriage' – and it *is* that by anybody's standards, but most particularly by those of Hollywood – was hard won and has been kept alive and well through a combination of mutual respect, growing wisdom and maturity and the art of compromise, as well as by shared commitments and moral values. Above all, this exceptional relationship has been cemented by true love that has stood the test of time.

It all began in 1952. Paul Newman, a talented young stage actor aged twenty-seven, had gradually been working his arduous way up the difficult ladder of the New York theatre via television appearances, small parts on Broadway, and the privilege of training at Lee Strasberg's famous Actors' Studio. Blessed with ability, a sharp intelligence and a rumbustious sense of humour, Newman had the added advantage of outstanding good looks. A fine physique and a wonderfully etched profile were further complemented by a pair of compelling, brilliantly blue eyes which, in years to come, would seduce cinema goers of all ages and both sexes throughout the world.

In 1952 the young actor got his first important break on Broadway. He was hired as an understudy to Ralph Meeker in William Inge's new play *Picnic*, directed by Joshua Logan. Shortly after rehearsals began, Logan decided to cast Paul in a small and rather thankless role, in which he nevertheless managed to attract notice. The play was an enormous success, running for fourteen months and playing 477 performances. In such circumstances, Paul could hardly avoid meeting the young actress who understudied both the female leads. Her name was Joanne Woodward. She was a slim, green-eyed blonde of what was to prove exceptional acting talent, and the pair found an instant rapport which was rapidly transformed into friendship.

Newman had already developed into a man of strong moral character, and was the husband of a former actress called Jacqueline Witte who had borne him a son. Paul and Jackie had met in the summer stock theatre company at Woodstock, Illinois, in 1949. He was at the very beginning of his career, having just completed his degree at college which he attended after having seen war service. They married at the end of that year and, soon afterwards, the death of Paul's father took the young couple to Cleveland, Ohio, Paul's family home, where he shouldered the responsibility of his late father's sporting goods business. He ran things efficiently but without interest or enthusiasm and, after a couple of years, the business was sold and Paul and Jackie went to New Haven to pick up the threads of their theatrical careers. After the birth of their baby, however, Jackie decided to give up her profession in order to devote herself fully to her family. They had two more children together, both daughters.

Joanne, by contrast, was a single girl with no commitments but, reading between the lines, it is obvious that this daughter of 'a Southern family of quality' (she was born and raised in Georgia) respected the Newman marriage. Although Joanne's own background was middle-class and supportive, her own parents had divorced, and this had made an unhappy impression on her. She would, therefore, have gone out of her way to avoid being the cause of distress to others and, as she was later to remark, she and Paul 'ran away from each other for six years'.

But fate had other plans. As a direct result of his appearance in *Picnic*, Newman was offered a contract in Hollywood with Warner Bros. Thus, in 1954, the up-and-coming stage actor arrived to join the film colony. But his was no instant success story. He was cast as the young Greek silversmith, Basil, in *The Silver Chalice*, a religious epic about the early Christians told in the best Hollywood style – or, one should say, the worst Hollywood style. The film was one of the most inept fiascos of the genre, and Newman himself wishes to this day that he could disown it. It is reported that he took one look at this hideous mess, duly flayed by the critics, and cabled his agent saying, 'Get me back on Broadway.' The studio allowed him to depart, but only at the price of a new contract that called for two films a year and the right to a third. Meanwhile, in February 1955, Paul opened on Broadway in a thriller called *The Desperate Hours*. He gave a very striking performance in the unpleasant guise of the psychopathic 'team leader' of three escaped convicts who terrorize a family in whose home they have taken refuge.

Far more momentous, however, than either *The Desperate Hours* or *The Silver Chalice* in Paul's life was the fact that, later in the year of his first Hollywood sojourn, Joanne Woodward was contracted by Twentieth Century-Fox studios and arrived for *her* first encounter with film making. While Paul went back to Broadway, returning to Hollywood to make a powerful but somewhat overlooked and now forgotten film *The Rack* (for which Warners were only too happy to lend him to M.G.M.), and then to score the first big success of his screen career as boxer Rocky Graziano in *Somebody Up There Likes Me*, Joanne was experiencing her own baptism of fire in the Dream Factory.

As with Paul's first film, Joanne's was a waste of her talent but, unlike *The Silver Chalice*, *Count Three And Pray*, in which she co-starred with Van Heflin, was not an appallingly bad film. It was a small-scale Western, a minor and over-sentimental piece, which passed by without too much notice. Her next two film roles saw the beginnings of a pattern that has continued, with one or two exceptions, to characterize her screen work ever since: she has almost invariably been the most striking ingredient of the films she.has appeared in, be the pictures good, bad, or indifferent, or her parts big or small.

In 1957, while Joanne Woodward was thus occupied, Paul Newman made two films which did nothing to advance his career: *The Helen Morgan Story* and *Until They Sail* (again on loan to M.G.M.). He needed a big film now if stardom were to come his way. Added to these professional frustrations, of course, was the strain of protecting his marriage under the pressure of constant separation from home, and the ever-present spectre of his deep friendship with Joanne Woodward.

Joanne, meanwhile, was given her first big break by producer–director Nunnally Johnson. But it did not come without a fight. Twentieth Century-Fox didn't know quite what to do with their talented contract player. She was not made in any obvious, easily recognizable mould for stardom and, besides, her intelligence and her fierce integrity gave her the strength to fight against the really poor roles which she was offered. The studio did not seem to have grasped the nature of her potential in her first three ventures so, when Johnson asked for her for the plum role of a triple schizophrenic, they said no. It was only after a stream of famous stars had turned down the offer that they relented.

And so it happened that Woodward, much less well-known than Newman but almost parallel with him in their screen careers, came to win the coveted Best Actress Oscar for only her fourth film, *The Three Faces Of Eve*.

Of course, nobody knew that Joanne Woodward was going to win the Academy Award until the following year, when she carried it off from some illustrious contenders. Meanwhile, she and Paul Newman co-starred in *The Long Hot Summer*, which began shooting late in 1957. It was a significant assignment for both of them. Paul, by now the father of three children, could not come to terms easily with the idea of dissolving his marriage and, in spite of the discretion with which he and Joanne conducted their friendship, the tongues of Hollywood were beginning to wag ever more loudly. It was at this time that Jackie Newman took the sad but considered decision to end the marriage, and it was with the final divorce proceedings under way that Paul and Joanne went on location to Mississippi to make a picture together for the first time. The knowledge that he would soon be free to pursue his relationship with Joanne openly must have brought Paul much comfort in his personal life but, professionally too, *The Long Hot Summer*, adapted from writings by William Faulkner and directed by Martin Ritt, was the break he had needed.

The Long Hot Summer gave Newman his first opportunity to dominate the screen with a powerful portrayal of an individual-istic loner – an outsider, always charming, sometimes ruthless. The loner was an area of characterization that the actor was to make very much his own over the years, most notably in *The Hustler* (1961), in *Hud* (1963), in *Cool Hand Luke* (1967) and, in his grizzled, remarkably handsome later years, *Absence Of Malice* (1981) and *The Verdict* (1982). For every one of these films, his brilliant work was acknowledged by an Academy Award nomination for Best Actor. The only statistical fact more startling than this is, that on each and every one of these occasions, the Academy saw fit to actually award the Oscar to somebody else.

For Paul and Joanne the year 1958 began professionally with another co-starring production, this time for television, in a well-received Playhouse 90 presentation, *The 80–Yard Run*. Both their performances were praised by the *New York Times* but, pleasing as this no doubt was, a rather more significant joint venture was begun on 29 January at the Hotel El Rancho Vegas in Las Vegas where, after six years of battling with the knowledge that they belonged together, Paul Newman and Joanne Woodward were finally married. Their overwhelming feeling was one of intense relief that the waiting was over, and they left for their honeymoon in Europe and England.

Their maturity of outlook was certainly to be put to the test in the years to come. Stardom, with its attendant pressures, was around the corner for Paul, while Joanne's career continued to be dogged by films (many of them, it must be said, in which her husband co-starred) that failed to make it really big at the box-office. She would also have to come to terms with playing second fiddle to Paul as a famous public figure although, ironically, she has always been the more outgoing and co-operative of the pair in giving press and television interviews and providing the quotable quotes that have lent an insight into their personalities and their relationship. There would also be the interruptions and responsibility of caring for a large family for Joanne, and, over the years, they have had to weather a certain amount of resentment against them in the Hollywood community.

But, sufficient to the moment, they returned from their honeymoon, which they had been able to enjoy in the freedom of still being relatively unknown and unrecognized, to begin married life. They settled down in Beverly Hills, like the majority of practically minded film actors, and Joanne's first personal problem as a wife was to forge a good relationship with Paul's three children by Jackie. They did not initially accept their new stepmother with uncomplicated enthusiasm but, as she would with all future difficulties, Joanne – already twenty-eight years old

113

at the time of her first and only marriage – overcame the problem in time. Another difficulty for the Newmans lay in the realization that they disliked living in Hollywood. As serious-minded people who were never deceived by the superficial glitter of the film colony, they did not find the lifestyle to their taste, and they were uncomfortable with the values that surrounded them. Indeed, Joanne viewed California as 'a beautiful woman dying of cancer', and was far happier with the more stable and less polluted environment of the east coast.

The couple dealt with this particular unease by acquiring a second home in beautiful rural Connecticut. An eighteenth-century converted coach house, it was to prove the perfect place in which to bring up their family, to meet congenially with their chosen friends, to house a veritable menagerie – dogs, cats, and even a horse named Tuppence – and, generally, to guard their cherished privacy away from the hurly-burly of their working lives. It was precisely this kind of desire for normalcy and a certain isolation from their colleagues that provoked resentment against them. As Joanne is on record as saying, 'We have our differences, but the outside world doesn't often get a chance to get inside our house.'

This constancy and self-containment has sometimes given the impression that Paul Newman and Joanne Woodward are rather a dull couple. Nothing could be farther from the truth. They both have a marvellous, sometimes self-deprecating sense of humour; they are adventurous and ambitious and unusual in their interests; they certainly have a refreshing ability frankly to acknowledge their own gifts, thereby exposing the ego and vanity common to actors, but without giving offence. And if they have chosen to distance themselves a little from the tiny, incestuous *milieu* of Hollywood, they nevertheless do number several actors and actresses (notably Robert Wagner and Robert Redford whom Paul particularly admires) among their good friends.

After they returned from their honeymoon in Europe, Paul went to Warners to star as Billy the Kid in *The Left-Handed Gun*, a modestly budgeted Western directed by Arthur Penn. He gave an excellent performance, but it was an otherwise uneven film that met with a mixed reception. Interestingly, the screenplay was based on a teleplay by the American writer and public figure Gore Vidal, to whom Joanne had become engaged for a time in the years when she and Paul were unable to be together. In an interview ten years after her marriage, Joanne said, 'I married late because I remembered what my great-grandmother told me about getting married: "Could you see yourself *talking* to him over breakfast for 50 years?" I can to Paul. The only other man was Gore Vidal, and we thought we would at least between us know all the Kings of England off by heart.'

Cat On A Hot Tin Roof won Paul his first Academy Award nomination and set him more markedly on the road to fame and fortune. It could not have done his standing any harm to co-star with Elizabeth Taylor, whose own performance was a testament to her courage as well as to her talent, for, only nine days into shooting *Cat On A Hot Tin Roof*, her much loved husband, Mike Todd, was killed in an aircrash, leaving her stricken with grief.

Newman's next film was undertaken with optimism for not only was it to bring him and his wife together on the screen again, but it was to provide an opportunity they both wanted to shift gear and play comedy. In the event, the experiment was a failure, with the critics almost wilfully overlooking the obvious gifts for comedy which Paul and Joanne did exhibit in *Rally Round The Flag Boys*, and virtually blaming them personally for its awfulness.

As a husband-and-wife team, the Newmans have not enjoyed a lot of success. The distinguished film writer David Shipman has observed, 'Such is the way that the publicity machines and fan magazines work, most husband-and-wife teams have been written up out of all proportion to the results on screen. In fact, very few married couples have been either prolific or successful as a team, and it is ironic that one of the most prolific – and most talented – should have been the least successful in commerical terms. Most of the films co-starring Paul Newman and Joanne Woodward have been poorly received, and she never *quite* made it on her own; had it not been for his commanding stellar status she might well have been forgotten long ago, lost in the wash with the many other intelligent and admired actresses who never quite came to terms with Hollywood stardom.' Shipman's analysis is perhaps a little harsh in that it is hard to credit that Joanne Woodward would ever have been 'forgotten' or 'lost in the wash'. She would certainly have become a serious and major Broadway star if she hadn't persevered with films, and some critics take the view that

she might have been better off if all her work had been independent of her illustrious husband. No one will ever know, but that
she didn't *quite* make it is true, and this created a strand of
difficulty in the marriage which only a lot of hard work and
understanding was to solve.

Joanne has expressed contradictory views about her professional partnership with her husband over the years, although
there is no argument anywhere that when he assumed the mantle
of her director rather than her co-star and made *Rachel, Rachel*
in 1967, they achieved a near-perfect and highly acclaimed little
work of art for which Joanne was justly nominated for an Oscar.
Looking back on that film now, one can only conclude that the
misfortune of bad scripts was what prevented Joanne Woodward
from becoming an international star.

In 1959, the second year of the Newman's marriage, Paul
starred in *The Young Philadelphians*, a well-made and entertaining soap-opera but hardly a milestone in the cinema, while Mrs
Newman was yet again called on to play women in the grip of
those baroque emotional upheavals which seem to inspire all
dramas set in the Deep South. In the aptly titled *The Sound And
The Fury*, she was teamed with Yul Brynner. Following hot on its
heels came a farrago of nymphomania, alcoholism, murder,
arson and terminal illness called *The Fugitive Kind*, in which
Joanne was co-starred with Marlon Brando. Unfortunately the
film was a critical disaster as well as a financial failure.

In March 1959 Paul opened in a new Broadway play, *Sweet
Bird Of Youth*, by the ubiquitous Tennessee Williams, directed
by Elia Kazan and co-starring the splendid Geraldine Page. It
was a fine play, and Newman and Page would recreate their
performances in the screen version. In the summer of that year,
Paul finally parted company with Warner Bros. He had never
been happy with the set-up and his most successful films had
been made when he was on loan to other studios, an arrange-
ment which brought substantial financial rewards to Warners but
not to their star. It is reputed that he paid the studio an enormous sum – in the region of half a million dollars – to purchase
his freedom, but the sense of relief was worth the sacrifice and,
besides, with his box-office appeal steadily rising, his future
earnings would soon offer generous compensation.

If the success of the play and his new independent status were landmarks of the Newman year, they were secondary to an important and joyous event in his private life. On 7 April 1959 Joanne gave birth to their first child, a daughter whom they named Elinor. The baby became known as Nell and, in due course, acquired an affectionate nickname, 'Nell Potts', which was to become known outside the family circle when she was billed under that name in *Rachel, Rachel*, playing her mother as a child. And then she made an impact as Joanne's daughter in *The Effect Of Gamma Rays On Man-In-The-Moon Marigolds*, an impressive family affair also directed by her father. A touching insight into Joanne's feelings about her husband and her daughter was provided when a television interviewer suggested to Joanne that Nell was more attractive than her mother. Joanne unhesitatingly responded to this provocation with, 'That is hardly surprising. My father wasn't Paul Newman.'

Paul stayed with *Sweet Bird Of Youth* until January of the following year though, towards the end of the run, he contrived to more or less be in two places at once, flying backwards and forwards between east and west coasts to commence shooting a new film by day while performing on stage at night. The film was another vehicle for both Newmans, and another artistic failure. *From The Terrace* was adapted from a bestselling novel by John O'Hara and might reasonably accurately be described as a cousin to *Dallas* and *Dynasty* in its social, sexual, psychological and financial concerns. Although it was badly received by the critics the stars delivered fine performances, particularly Joanne who, for once, was permitted to look chic and attractive; and, not before time, this one was at least a success at the box-office.

When *From The Terrace* was finished, all three Newmans left for Israel where Paul was to play Jewish freedom fighter Ari Ben-Canaan in Otto Preminger's sprawling, chaotic version of *Exodus*. (Paul is himself half-Jewish – the paternal half – and half Roman Catholic.) The film is generally regarded as dreadful and Paul, who did not see eye to eye with the notoriously difficult Preminger, was unhappy making it, but he collected a cool $200,000 by way of a pay-cheque. By now he could truly be said to have arrived as a major film star. He was rich, he was famous, he was a box-office draw, and he had the added bonus of a happy marriage. But his artistic aspirations and sense of challenge were undernourished. He needed to make a film that would both satisfy his own high standards and stand up to critical appraisal.

These aspirations were met with his next film, *The Hustler*. Beautifully directed by Robert Rossen, this work has grown in reputation over the years, and is being re-shown in the 1980s as a classic of its kind. As Eddie Felson, the hard-drinking, drifting, ruthless con-man obsessed by his desire to become a living legend as the best pool player ever, Newman gave a brilliant performance of real stature. Eddie is one of the great Newman loners – tough and tender, charming and cynical by turns – but the star lost out in the Oscar stakes to Maximilian Schell in *Judgment At Nuremberg*.

In his excellent biography of Paul Newman, Lionel Godfrey offers a fascinating analysis of star quality and says of Newman that he is ' ... a star whom it was easy to admire and with whom it was natural to sympathise; but not one who ever really seemed like the common man or the boy next door. It was to be left to such stars as Michael Caine and Dustin Hoffman, following the example set by the earlier William Holden, to reduce to vanishing point the gap between stars and public. With his jealously guarded private life ... and his roles that defied simple identification, Paul Newman was arguably one of the last stars. As a person he retained an aura of mystery and withdrawal. As a screen symbol, he was almost always an outsider or one who would end up as an outcast or martyr – an aliented modern hero. What *The Hustler* had almost ideally refined, the rest of his career would repeat and consolidate. The inaccessibility of both man and star would continue to be a potent ingredient in the Newman chemistry.'

The potent ingredients in the chemistry of the Newman marriage, however, were somewhat different. Aside from the evident love, attraction and respect they felt for each other, there was the large matter of coming to terms with each other's differences, while building on their common ground. Joanne has said, 'The real cement in our marriage is that we have developed a similarity of attitudes to living and a commitment to the same things in life.' Besides which, as she has also commented, 'The thing is we *like* each other.' They were learning to accommodate each other's markedly dissimilar personalities and pursuits on the one hand, and the professional imbalance between them on the other. From the latter test Joanne Woodward, who, in a sense, had to bear the brunt of the disparity, has emerged with flying colours, overcoming career frustrations, enduring long separations from her husband when he was away filming in the company of beautiful women, shouldering the burdens of home and family, and playing second fiddle to Paul's public image.

Joanne has recognized and defined her difficulties with rare insight and honesty, acknowledging their temperamental differences while always remaining generous in her assessment of Paul. ' ... he is more beautiful than I am. He improves in beauty as he grows older. I can fake beauty or be a plain old shoe. I'm like a female Alec Guinness – easy to pass by in the street with people unaware of who we are.' She has acknowledged that ' ... Paul is a bigger star than I am and of course it is irritating when your husband is called a sex symbol or a superstar because the reality and the belief tend to get blurred.'

In 1963, however, the really difficult patch still lay ahead, though their lives were not without controversy and hard decisions. On the credit side, their second daughter, Melissa, had been born, and Paul's latest film, *Hud*, very much a cousin in flavour to *The Hustler*, was released to acclaim. Also released was *The Stripper*, a vehicle for Joanne in a starring role which had originally been intended for Marilyn Monroe, but in which Joanne distinguished herself. She displayed all of her rich interpretive qualities and captured what critic Pauline Kael described as 'the right forlorn gallantry' of Lila, the stripper of the title. It was an excellent, if flawed, film, and it is hard to see why it did little to raise Joanne's status.

The Newmans' division of homes between Beverly Hills and Connecticut finally ended, with the decision to base themselves full-time in the latter. In abandoning the Beverly Hills house, they naturally refuelled the hostility of those who regarded the distancing as a slight.

That hostility, however, was secondary to the unpopularity in certain quarters brought about by the Newmans' political affiliations. Political allegiances among entertainers in Hollywood have, with some exceptions, tended towards the conservative, and it was really only in the late 1960s that a vociferous band of liberals, notably Jane Fonda, began to trumpet their views without reserve. Paul and Joanne were, therefore, fairly early film-star liberals and, as in the other important and personal areas of their lives, conducted themselves with restraint. However, in 1963 their politics were made public when Paul, in company with Anthony Franciosa, Marlon Brando and Virgil Frye, went to Alabama to attend a rally on racialism led by Martin Luther King. Already that year Paul had involved himself with a civil rights march to Washington and a sit-in protesting against the housing situation in Sacramento. Five years later, he campaigned for Senator Eugene McCarthy in the presidential race and was a delegate to the Democratic convention. Both Newmans remain committed to fighting for liberal causes, whether they be environmental, nuclear, poverty or race issues, and it is alarming to realize that this has engendered resentment rather than admiration in Hollywood. Indeed, some suspect that it is Paul's politics which deprived him of winning an Academy Award, and of even a nomination for directing *Rachel, Rachel*, an omission Joanne termed 'reprehensible' and which, given the fact that this superb film was nominated in every other major category, has to be seen, rightly or wrongly, as an intentional snub to the man who made it. (In 1986 Paul was belatedly awarded an honorary Oscar for his collected achievements.)

Rachel, Rachel, released in 1968, in fact proved to be the apogee of Joanne Woodward's career. As Rachel, the small-town schoolteacher consigned to spinsterhood, whose life is changed by her first, late, and temporary, experience of a love affair, she displayed the full and perfect range of her gifts. She won the *New York Times* Critics' Award for Best Actress and was nominated for the Oscar (she lost out to Katharine Hepburn in *The Lion In Winter*). The film itself gained a Best Picture nomination, losing out to, of all things, the musical *Oliver!*, and it was a big box-office success as well as a critical triumph. *Rachel, Rachel* was a significant event in Paul's life. He had undertaken the project in a conscious bid to inject new life into his wife's flagging career, and succeeded, which was important to their partnership both personally and professionally. In addition, by proving his flair in the director's role, he opened up new fields to conquer.

In the 1960s, prior to her success in *Rachel, Rachel*, Joanne Woodward had made only seven pictures – two of them with her husband – and none of them a hit. The most important event in her life during those years occurred in April 1965, when she gave birth to their third and last child, another daughter, whom they christened Claire, but called Clea. Paul, in the same number of years, had made seventeen films. They were a mixed bag, numbering a few failures but, as well as *The Hustler* and *Hud*, they included *Hombre* and *Cool Hand Luke*, both strikingly good, and *Harper*, a huge box-office hit for his old studio, Warner Bros., in which he portrayed a greatly appealing private eye. The decade had seen Paul Newman enter the official box-office Top Ten for the first time in 1963. He came in at number nine and stayed there the following year, then disappeared off the list in 1965. In 1966 he re-entered in the same position but rose to fifth place in 1967, made it to number two in 1968, and ended the decade listed at number one, a place he occupied again in 1970.

The 1960s ended with a sour note on the personal front. The marriage came in for unsympathetic gossip and rumour from time to time, almost as though a segment of the Hollywood community actually wished the Newmans ill. It was, of course, all grist to the mill of the lower-grade columnists and it seemed that, as the couple's general public image collected ever more respect and admiration for their artistic achievements, political principles and impeccable private life, the flames of jealousy and envy burned higher. Finally, in a fit of angry hurt and frustration, Paul and Joanne took out a half-page advertisement in the *Los Angeles Times* stating, 'We are not breaking up.' This more or less silenced the gossip mongers until a new wave of tasteless and unfounded rumour broke again for a while in the mid-1970s. That time round, Paul and Joanne ignored it. 1969 saw the release of the staggeringly successful *Butch Cassidy And The Sundance Kid*, the film which ensured that Paul would start the next decade as big a star as he would ever be.

During the 1970s the quantity (and quality) of film work undertaken by the Newmans diminished somewhat, and Paul's enthusiasm for motor-racing began to occupy him on an ever larger scale. Like his friend and colleague Steve McQueen, he developed his passion into a really serious pursuit and, in 1974, had become sufficiently expert to win two national championships, driving a Datsun. Joanne's reaction to the sport has been variously reported as for and against. According to Paul, talking at the age of fifty-seven when most men would have abandoned racing, Joanne ' ... loves it. She saw it gave me a different kind of focus on life and got the fires going again.'

Joanne's interests are very different. She is a ballet fanatic and not only as audience. She took it up for her own satisfaction when in her mid-thirties. She also pursues, with characteristic energy and commitment, horse-riding, the study of languages, philosophy, the piano, and participates in women's conferences on such issues as examining the implications of nuclear war. But in spite of her amazing resources and her genuine devotion to raising her family, the 1970s were not a particularly happy time for Mrs Paul Newman. She went into semi-retirement for a few years and says, 'Those years when I wasn't working were lousy. I didn't enjoy it and neither did the girls. I tried to be a model homemaker but it wasn't very productive for anyone.'

Paul directed *Sometimes A Great Notion*, starring Lee Remick. It didn't succeed and the majority of films in which he starred were at best mediocre. The two highlights of these years both came early in the decade. In 1972 he again directed his wife, this time in a screen adaptation of the stage hit, *The Effect Of Gamma Rays On Man-In-The-Moon Marigolds* – an unwieldy title which might partly have accounted for its lack of commercial success. However, it was critically well-received and, *Rachel, Rachel* proved yet again the potency of teaming the talented Newmans on opposite sides of the camera. It was beautifully directed, Joanne was superb and daughter Nell Potts almost stole the show. In 1973 came *The Sting*, reuniting Paul and Robert Redford in a bid to repeat the success of *Butch Cassidy*. It did.

Towards the end of the 1970s Joanne's career shifted steadily away from the big screen to the stage and television, where she has enjoyed conspicuous success. In 1977 she went to England to play in a TV version of William Inge's *Come Back Little Sheba*, co-starring with Sir Laurence Olivier.

The 1980s have slowed down considerably for Paul and Joanne. They space out their work and live quietly, seeing good friends in their New York apartment. Joanne is a fine cook and Paul, it would seem, is no stranger to the kitchen. Famous among friends for his salad dressing, he decided, more as a gag than anything else, to market it. Today, 'Newman's Own' is a million-dollar-a-year concern, the profits of which Paul gives to charity. However, if he no longer makes films in quantity, they are certainly back on course where quality is concerned. He distinguished himself in both *Absence Of Malice* and, particularly, *The Verdict*. In 1983 he directed a film called *Harry And Son*, about a father-and-son relationship. The experience must have been deeply poignant for Paul who, in 1978, lost his only son, Scott, who died at the age of twenty-eight from a drugs overdose. It is a topic the Newmans do not discuss, but they set up the Scott Newman Foundation, dedicated to educating children to an awareness of the dangers of drug-taking.

As the decade marches on, it is astounding to realize that Paul Newman and Joanne Woodward, still very active, are aged sixty-three and fifty-eight respectively, and have been married for thirty years. It hasn't always been easy. Joanne, after twenty-five years of married life, phrased it thus, 'The idea that we have some kind of perfect marriage is absurd. We seem constantly to be projected as an ideal couple and wonderful parents. It isn't true and it's a terrible burden to carry around. It also makes us seem fairly humourless and rather dull, which I don't think we are.'

If their years together have called on their reserves of understanding, they have certainly not been boring. As Paul remarked, 'I never know who I'm going to meet in the morning. Living with her is sometimes startling, frequently difficult, but never dull.'

How, then, have they succeeded where so many have failed? According to Joanne, 'There is sensible compromise. I hate flying but I will fly to be with him when he is working somewhere. I hate skiing, but I go on skiing holidays just to be able to have dinner with him at night. He hates ballet but he'll come because I like it, and he'll listen when I tell him how a pianist plays at a concert.'

Paul sums it up thus, 'We live in a throwaway society. We throw away bottles and cans and children and wives and marriages. But Joanne and I work at ours. We fix the toaster if it breaks, and we fix our marriage too when it is strained.'

What they both might have added is that no compromise can work without love. Paul Newman and Joanne Woodward may not be the most superficially glamorous couple in the history of Hollywood, but they provide one of its rare true love stories. Long may it continue.

CLARK GABLE
— AND —
CAROLE LOMBARD

'Why did Ma have to go?' a grief-stricken Clark Gable kept repeating after the tragic death of his wife Carole Lombard on 16 January 1942. 'Did you ever see anyone more beautiful? There never was a person in this world who was so generous, so full of fun. God damn it, why Ma?'

Shock-waves reverberated around the world at the news that the gorgeous, glamorous and gifted star had been killed in the very prime of her life. President Franklin D. Roosevelt, in a condolence telegram to Gable, said, 'She is, and always will be, a star, one we shall never forget nor cease to be grateful to.' Millions of fans mourned the passing of an actress whose sparkling personality and scintillating comic timing can still be marvelled at in such films as *My Man Godfrey, Nothing Sacred* and *To Be Or Not To Be*. But Clark Gable, Hollywood's most famous handsome male star, known as 'the King', who had loved Lombard and shared the last few years of her life, continued to mourn her until he joined her almost eighteen years later.

They first met in 1932 when, for the first and last time, they were co-starred on screen – in *No Man Of Her Own* at Paramount. It was a far from passionate working relationship. Each was preoccupied with their personal problems: Carole's marriage to William Powell was heading for the rocks and Clark, although still married to wealthy socialite Ria Langham, had lost his heart to Joan Crawford. Despite the stars affectionately nicknaming each other 'Ma' and 'Pa' on the set, Carole thought Clark rather stuffy and reserved, while he objected to her swearing and what he saw as her inflated ego. At the end of filming she presented him with a large smoked ham bearing his portrait, and he gave her a pair of ballet shoes.

125

The romance caught fire four years later at a typically Hollywood party of the Thirties, whacky and extravagant. It was an all-white affair: the women wore white, the men were clad in white tie and tails; the footmen were dressed in white, and the ballroom was decorated with showers of white roses and gardenias. The blonde Lombard looked ravishing in her flimsy white gown, and Gable found himself flashing his famous smile and asking her to dance. Seeing each other again in this alabaster setting seemed to ignite a mutual attraction. 'I go for you, Ma,' he said. 'I go for you too, Pa,' she replied. Carole's marriage to Powell had ended in 1933 and Clark was now legally separated from his wife. They danced to the appropriate strains of 'Cheek to Cheek', and Gable offered to drive Lombard home in his Dusenberg convertible. In fact he drove to the Beverly Wilshire Hotel where he was living and invited her up for a nightcap. 'Who do you think you are? Clark Gable?' she said by way of refusal. It was rare for women to turn down Hollywood's hottest heart-throb.

The next morning a pair of doves in a gilded cage were delivered to Clark's room. Tied to the leg of one of the birds was a tag which read, 'How about it? – Carole.' Amused and encouraged, he responded accordingly and they began dating. The well-built, virile Gable was accustomed to being pursued by women, but Lombard, contrary to her outward frivolity, needed more than a meaningless flirtation. She was looking for a long-term relationship. Few people took the affair seriously in the beginning – she was reckless and impulsive, he was a womanizer – but gradually it became clear that the couple were head over heels in love and nothing would stop them. Not for the first time did Hollywood provide an environment in which two people from vastly differing backgrounds met and fell in love.

William Clark Gable was born in the little mining town of Cadiz, Ohio on 1 February 1901. His mother died nine months after his birth and he was brought up by a firm but loving stepmother. He left school at fourteen to work in a tyre factory and then joined his father, an oil-driller, on the Oklahoma oil fields until he reached his majority. Finding himself penniless in Oregon, he took a variety of labouring jobs before becoming involved with a travelling theatre company. The future screen idol was then a gangling youth with large hands and feet, a thin face that made his prominent jug ears stick out all the more, and front teeth that were both crooked and decaying. Still only twenty-one, he met an actress and drama teacher named Josephine Dillon who was fourteen years his senior. Josephine coached him in acting, worked on his voice, taught him to move with grace and paid to have his teeth fixed. In 1924 they moved to Los Angeles where they married. His new status didn't stop Clark from involving himself with other women, very often older women in a position to advance his career. One such was wealthy forty-three-year-old Ria Langham, who had numbered a Texan oil millionaire among her three husbands. She taught Gable the social graces and used her connections to get him work on the New York stage which, in turn, led him to a contract with M.G.M. Now divorced from Josephine and warned by studio boss Louis B. Mayer to stay away from Joan Crawford (his co-star in *Dance, Fools, Dance* and the then wife of Douglas Fairbanks Jr), Clark decided to marry Ria in March 1931.

Carole Lombard was born Alice Jane Peters on 6 October 1908, the daughter of well-to-do, educated parents. Mr and Mrs Peters separated in 1915 and Carole was taken to live in Los Angeles with her mother and two brothers. An attractive child, she had her first screen job at the age of twelve. After completing junior high school she enrolled in drama classes and in 1925 returned to films as blonde ingenue Carol (the 'e' was added later) Lombard. But tragedy always seemed to stalk a few paces behind this girl who loved life. At eighteen she was thrown against the windscreen of a car and suffered a deep cut along her left cheek to the corner of her mouth. The surgeon warned of the danger that her muscles would relax under an anaesthetic and leave her permanently disfigured. She reacted by gritting her teeth and submitting to fourteen stitches being sewn into her cheek without anything to relieve the pain. The incident epitomized the gutsy nature for which Lombard was so admired. While making *Man Of The World* in 1931, Carole fell in love with her leading man, the suave William Powell who was sixteen years her senior. They married in June and divorced a little over two years later, remaining good friends. A free woman, Carole had a romance with dark and handsome bandleader Russ Columbo, but tragedy struck again. Talk of marriage was in the air when Columbo was accidentally shot dead in 1934 at the age of twenty-six.

Slowly and surely throughout 1936 the love affair between Gable and Lombard blossomed and bloomed. Both were fashion-

127

plate dressers and made a spectacularly glamorous pair when out on the town, which was often. The celebrated costume designer Irene, who created most of Lombard's professional and personal wardrobe, commented, 'Whenever I'm asked to name the most exciting woman I've ever dressed, I say Carole.... Everything looked good on that beautiful figure. She knew clothes, and she knew how to wear them.' By now Carole had established herself as 'America's Madcap Playgirl Number One' on the screen and off, in contrast to Clark, who had grown rather stiff during his marriage to Ria with whom he had led a formal and snobbish social life. The witty, charming and carefree Carole, with her taste for practical jokes and her outrageously crude language, helped him to unbend. Laughter underlined almost everything they did together, yet Gable resisted getting a divorce. He was already paying Ria enormous chunks of his salary and simply couldn't face the financial sacrifice a divorce would entail. Like many people who work their way up from nothing, he was highly conscious of the value of money. In any event, as far as he was concerned he and Carole were husband and wife in all but name; of course they had to be seen to preserve the conventions of the day by maintaining separate establishments, but in fact they lived together in Bel-Air.

On a balmy June day in 1937 Gable and Lombard, both dressed in black, wearing dark glasses and visibly shaken, attended the funeral of Jean Harlow. Clark had been filming *Saratoga* with 'the Blonde Bombshell' when she was stricken, aged twenty-six, with a fatal illness. With hundreds of noisy fans swarming over Forest Lawn to gawp at their screen idols, the funeral was not a pretty sight. 'Don't let this happen when I go, Pa,' Carole whispered to Clark, holding his hand tightly. Soon afterwards she stated in her will that her funeral was to be private, with only family and intimate friends present. Did she sense it was to be only a mere five years later? 'I can never see into the future at all, I'm too busy living every day,' Carole told writer Adela Rogers St Johns. 'I'm not afraid of growing old, but I never see myself growing old.' She seldom spoke of any plans beyond the immediate future. All she was certain of was that she wanted to be Clark Gable's wife.

Her dream was finally realized when Gable accepted a large salary, plus a bonus of $100,000, to play Rhett Butler in *Gone*

With The Wind and felt he could now afford an expensive divorce. The decree was granted in March 1939 and Clark and Carole decided to marry immediately. Wanting a simple, publicity-free wedding, 'The King Of Hollywood' and 'The Screwball Queen Of The Screen' eloped to a small town in Arizona. There they were married at the house of the Episcopalian minister, whose wife and an excited neighbour were the witnesses. Mr and Mrs Gable drove back to Hollywood the same night, giggling like two school-children who had played truant. The next morning they announced their joyful news to the press, and Carole told columnist Louella Parsons that, 'I'll work for a few more years and then I want a family. I'll let Pa be the star and I'll stay home, darn the socks and look after the kids.' The couple bought a comfortable, homely, twenty-acre ranch in the San Fernando valley, and settled down to a life of genuine marital bliss. 'I've always wanted a place like this,' Clark told Carole. 'It will be the first home that I've had since I was a boy that I can really call my own. I think we're going to be happy here.' And Carole made sure that they were. She supervized the renovations and the interior decorating with Clark's tastes in mind. Her aim was to make the ranch into 'a man's home' and, when the work was completed, she said to her husband, with love and pride, 'Well, old King, you've finally got your castle.' At the ranch, punningly called 'The House of the Two Gables', they spent their time relaxing peacefully, deeply in love. Although huge earners, the Gables lived frugally by Hollywood standards, enjoying their rustic life. Clark pottered about the land, ploughing the fields and planting trees, while Carole fed the chickens and gardened. He loved to hunt, shoot and fish, and she learned to love it too. Also in residence on the ranch were dozens of doves, raised from the pair that Carole had given Clark at the beginning of their relationship.

In 1939 Lombard was again reminded of her own mortality. Just before embarking on her role as a nurse in *Vigil In The Night*, she was rushed into hospital with acute appendicitis. Clark remained at the hospital throughout and, although she was soon her old self, clowning with the doctors and nurses, she instantly drew up a new will making her husband her executor and major beneficiary. Only a few months later, when they were flying back together from a hunting expedition, the overloaded private amphibian plane in which they were travelling narrowly missed hitting the treetops.

This experience prompted Carole to plead with Clark, 'Please let's never travel in separate planes. Whenever I fly, I want you with me.'

Carole Lombard's New Year resolution for 1940 was to have a baby but this ambition eluded her. After consulting many doctors it was concluded that childbearing, though very difficult for her, was not impossible. It seems likely that Clark, too, took medical tests, but M.G.M. could in no circumstances afford to reveal that the virility of the country's leading male sex symbol might be in question. Meanwhile, it was common knowledge that Clark, though utterly devoted and emotionally faithful to his wife, tended to prove his virility elsewhere from time to time. Lombard tolerated these flings up to a point, but when Gable was cast opposite his old flame Joan Crawford in *Strange Cargo* Carole threatened to arrive on the set with a loaded shotgun if she heard any rumours. Nobody doubted that she was quite capable of doing so! In the summer of 1941 there was talk of Gable making a play for M.G.M.'s newest blonde sex goddess, twenty-one-year-old Lana Turner, during the making of *Honky Tonk*. Lombard invaded Louis B. Mayer's office, swearing to cause havoc should there be any scandal concerning her spouse and Turner, and thereafter visited the set regularly to make sure there was no hanky panky on *Honky Tonk*!

After a year's professional inactivity Carole returned to films, starring opposite Jack Benny in Ernst Lubitsch's brilliant anti-Nazi comedy *To Be Or Not To Be* but after the bombing of Pearl Harbor she wanted to do more than that for the war effort. Remembering old newsreels showing Mary Pickford, Douglas Fairbanks and Charlie Chaplin touring the country to sell war bonds during World War One, Carole wrote to President Roosevelt suggesting that she and her colleagues do the same. Clark, who was over draft age, became chairman of the Hollywood Victory Committee, organizing rallies and meetings to collect for the war effort. When the state of Indiana asked the committee to send a film star to promote the campaign, Gable nominated his wife for the job. It was a decision he would regret for the rest of his life.

Carole was thrilled to be able to do good in her native state. She wanted Clark to make the trip with her and was furious to learn that he couldn't because M.G.M. had re-teamed him with

Lana Turner for *Somewhere I'll Find You*, about to begin shooting. Clark suggested she take her mother instead. He did not see his wife off at Union Station on 12 January 1942 because they had quarrelled over his making the film with Lana. However, that night he found a naked tailor's dummy in his bed, complete with blonde wig and a note from Carole pinned to it reading, 'I'm Lana Turner's stand-in.' He burst out laughing and their differences were quickly patched up on the telephone. Carole in fact called him from every stop *en route* to Indianapolis.

Carole Lombard ended her exhausting tour by attending a victory rally in Indianapolis where she led the audience in singing 'The Star-Spangled Banner.' Then Fate played its cruel hand. Anxious to get back to Gable as quickly as possible, Lombard decided to fly home. Her companions, M.G.M. press agent Otto Winkler and her mother Mrs Peters, were against it – Otto suffered from air sickness, Mrs Peters, who had never flown before, was superstitious and an astrologer had told her not to fly in 1942. They agreed to settle the matter on the toss of a coin, and an ecstatic Carole was the victor. They managed to get seats on a T.W.A. flight leaving at 4 a.m., but when Mrs Peters, a great believer in numerology, realized the date would be 16 January, she told her daughter that sixteen was the sign of impending doom. A further indication of disaster, according to Carole's mother, was the recurrence of the number 'three'. The plane was a DC-3, there were three in the party, and Lombard was thirty-three years old. Carole did what she could to quieten her mother's fears but she would not be dissuaded from the journey. At a stop at Albuquerque T.W.A. asked Lombard's party whether they would give up their seats to three army officers who had been ordered urgently back to California. Carole didn't want to wait for the next plane and others disembarked instead. After refuelling at Las Vegas they took off again into a clear blue sky. A few minutes later the DC-3 crashed into the side of a mountain. There were no survivors.

Back at the ranch Clark was preparing a homecoming party for his wife. He had arranged red roses in every room and lit the house with candles. In Carole's bed he had placed a well-endowed male dummy in answer to her parting shot. At around 8.30 p.m. the phone rang and Gable was informed of the disaster; search parties, he was told, were on their way to the scene, and there was still hope. He left immediately for Las Vegas on a chartered plane and, on arrival, sped directly to the sheriff's office. The area of the crash had been located. 'How do you know the plane is there?' asked Gable. 'Because it's on fire,' replied the deputy. 'The flames shot up two or three hundred feet.'

The only traces found of the sublime Carole Lombard were a few wisps of hair and the diamond and ruby ear-clips Clark had given her at Christmas barely three weeks earlier. The heart-shaped ruby pendant she always wore, also a gift from Clark, was nowhere to be seen. Legend has it that it was embedded in her own heart by the impact of the crash. The distraught Gable spent the night in a bungalow, pacing the floor and chain-smoking. The next morning he was taken to see the wreck for himself, the final painful confirmation that his beloved was no more.

President Roosevelt wanted to honour Carole Lombard with a full military funeral, but Clark insisted that her request for a simple and private ceremony be carried out to the letter. After the funeral Gable broke down. He remained in a state of shock for several weeks, roaming the ranch alone, re-running Carole's films, thumbing through her scrapbooks. He drank heavily in an attempt to numb the grief and pain. After a time he somehow managed to go back to work and complete the picture he was making, then he announced he was going to enlist. At the age of forty-one Clark Gable became a gunner in the Army Air Force and saw action overseas. In October 1943 he was awarded the Distinguished Flying Cross and the Air Medal for bravery. He commented afterwards, 'I saw so much in the way of death and destruction that I realized that I hadn't been singled out for grief. I saw that others were suffering and losing their loved ones just as I lost Ma.'

The remaining years of Gable's life were spent searching for another Lombard, trying desperately to recapture something of what he had lost. The women he dated were all blonde, all witty, all reminiscent of Carole in some way. In 1949 he married Douglas Fairbanks Sr's widow, Sylvia, Lady Ashley. A blue-eyed blonde of forty-one – the age Carole would have been – she shared some of her predecessor's looks and high spirits, but not her understanding of Clark. Sylvia found it impossible to live in Carole's shadow and set about changing the character of the ranch. Not surprisingly, the marriage was a failure, lasting a little over a year. While making *Mogambo* Gable was attracted to Grace Kelly, who reminded him of Carole in certain ways, but the young beauty was meant for a different destiny. When another Lombard type, former model and actress Kay Williams, married Clark in July 1955, she determined not to fight Carole's ghost, but to emulate her as far as possible. They eloped, called each other Ma and Pa, and lived in the same way at the ranch; Kay dressed, behaved and swore as much like Carole as she could, and Gable found a degree of happiness in the illusion.

During the filming of *The Misfits* in Nevada, in the shadow of the mountain where Lombard was killed, Kay informed her fifty-nine-year-old husband that he was to become a father for the first time. 'Imagine a wonderful thing like this happening to an old guy like me. It's an extra dividend from life and I want to make the most of it.' Sadly, he never lived to see his son. In November 1960, four months before the birth of the baby, 'the King' died of a heart attack. He was laid to rest for ever beside Carole Lombard, his eternal love.

KATHARINE HEPBURN
— AND —
SPENCER TRACY

t around 6 a.m. on Saturday, 10 June 1967, just fifteen days after the film *Guess Who's Coming To Dinner?* had been completed, Spencer Tracy had a massive heart attack and died while drinking milk in the kitchen of his home. Katharine Hepburn found him a short time later hunched over the kitchen table. She telephoned the doctor, their friend George Cukor, and Tracy's brother Carroll, who in turn contacted Tracy's wife, Louise. Tracy was moved to the bedroom, where Kate sat alone with him. Ten minutes later she emerged, her eyes moist with tears, and walked out of the house.

Kate was not among the congregation that crowded into the Immaculate Heart of Mary Roman Catholic Church to hear the requiem mass held for Tracy, or among the hundreds of people at the burial at Forest Lawn Cemetery. While Louise stood at the graveside, veiled and in black, Kate remained at home in seclusion. Forty-eight hours later she went to offer her condolences to Louise and flew back to her family's summer home on the east coast for peace and consolation.

They seemed an ill-assorted couple, the embodiment of the theory of the attraction of opposites. He was a devout Catholic, she was a free-thinker; he was hard drinking, she was virtually a teetotaller; he was a physical wreck, she was a superb sportswoman; he was of Irish stock born in Milwaukee, Wisconsin, she was the WASP personified born in Hartford, Connecticut; he was a pessimist, she was an optimist; his acting talent lay in doing as little as possible, her style was showy.

On the other hand, Tracy and Hepburn shared the same brand of dry wit and humour, were equally dedicated to their chosen craft and could not tolerate flatterers or sycophants. They both had a no-nonsense attitude to life, did not suffer fools gladly, shunned publicity as much as possible, led extremely private lives, and held strong convictions. Each was a Democrat and a great admirer of Franklin D. Roosevelt, and they were repelled by the McCarthy witchhunts of the 1950s. They loved reading, music and the theatre, were interested in sports, enjoyed discussing politics, and had the same intellectual curiosity. They painted together – seascapes, landscapes, and scenes through the windows of their hotel bedrooms. They fulfilled each other intellectually, artistically and spiritually. It was a love affair that was sustained and unwavering, through good and bad times, from 1941 to Tracy's death in 1967 and beyond. And yet, although rumours filtered through, the public at large was never fully aware of the intensity of their relationship until the early 1970s. It was symptomatic of the respect and awe in which the two stars were held both by the press and by filmgoers that, even in the backbiting Hollywood *milieu*, no mud was ever slung at them.

When Katharine Hepburn was one of a list of stars labelled 'box office poison' in 1938 by a survey of film theatre owners, she left Hollywood for Broadway to play the lead in *The Philadelphia Story*, a part especially written for her by Philip Barry. Having paid twenty-five per cent of the production costs, she wisely waived her salary in exchange for a cut of the profits and the film rights. The play was a hit, so when M.G.M. made a bid for it, Hepburn held a trump card. She sold it to them on condition that she would not only star, but would have final approval of screenplay, director, and co-stars. Her first choice for the role of C. K. Dexter Haven (played on stage by Joseph Cotten), the ex-husband of spoiled society girl Tracy Lord (Hepburn), was Spencer Tracy. Although they had never met, Kate idolized Tracy on screen. She admired his skill in not seeming to act at all, his directness and simplicity, his quiet humour and warm personality, his masculine qualities, and his rugged yet sensitive features. She had seen most of his pictures and, above all, cherished his role as Manuel, the Portuguese fisherman, in *Captains Courageous* (1937). 'I can never face the end without weeping so!' she said after having seen it countless times. When neither Tracy, nor M.G.M.'s top money-making attraction Clark Gable, was available, Cary Grant took the role. Yet the success of the picture gave her new bargaining power and led to her celebrated meeting with Spencer Tracy.

When Kate went to M.G.M. with the script of *Woman Of The Year* in the summer of 1941, she insisted, as she owned the rights, that she would not sell it unless Spencer Tracy co-starred with her. However Tracy was in Florida on location for *The Yearling* and would not be free for some time. Then the unexpected happened. For various reasons *The Yearling* was postponed and Tracy was now willing and able to make the film opposite Hepburn. He admired her grace and style. After seeing *The Philadelphia Story* he proclaimed her 'a damn fine actress' and suggested to Louis B. Mayer that she play both female leads in his *Dr Jekyll And Mr Hyde*, an idea Mayer immediately rejected. However, Tracy was slightly wary of Hepburn's reputation for being uppity and her habit of wearing trousers in public. She was in awe of the man she was about to meet, although she had heard tales of his drinking and womanizing.

Hepburn at five feet seven inches was tall for a Hollywood actress, and with four-inch platform shoes, her hair piled high on her head and her rigid back, she seemed far taller. Tracy was a big man but not particularly tall at five feet ten and a half inches. On their first meeting, when the film's producer Joseph L. Mankiewicz introduced them, Kate remarked, 'I'm afraid I'm a little tall for you, Mr Tracy.' On seeing Spencer's abashed look, Mankiewicz quipped, 'Don't worry, baby, he'll soon cut you down to size.' After she left, Tracy turned to Mankiewicz and said, 'Not me, boy, I don't want to get mixed up with anything like that.' Later, when she asked Tracy what he thought of the script, he replied, 'It's all right. Not much for me to do as it stands – but Shorty, you better watch yourself in the clinches!' It was the beginning of a beautiful friendship.

Up to the time of filming *Woman Of The Year* Kate had been dating director George Stevens, who resembled Tracy physically, for about six months. When she stipulated that Stevens direct the picture there was speculation that marriage might be in the offing but as soon as shooting got under way, something remarkable happened between Hepburn and Tracy. As the camera began to turn, it acted upon them like a magic ray: they fell in love. People around them and those working on the picture began to notice small things. In the first few days Tracy had called Hepburn 'Shorty' or 'That woman', but it gradually became 'Kate' or 'Kath'. She seemed to glow with a new feminine aura, and though she always wore slacks or jeans she seemed to take more care over her appearance. Stevens recognized the symptoms and backed away from his romantic attachment in a gentlemanly manner. On the very first day of shooting Kate's acting was subdued, her usually clear and distinctive diction was mumbled. Tracy spoke his lines in an artificial and overstudied manner. 'My God!' cried Mankiewicz. 'They're imitating each other!' Stevens noted that 'From the beginning of the picture, and their relationship, Spence's reaction to her was a total, pleasant but glacial put-down of her extreme effusiveness. He just didn't get disturbed about doing things immediately; she wanted to do a hundred and one things at once; he was never in a hurry.'

Woman Of The Year proved to be one of the top earners of the 1941–2 season. *Time* magazine wrote that 'Actors Hepburn and Tracy have a fine old time. ... They take turns playing straight for each other, act one superbly directed love scene ... ', and the *Baltimore Sun* recognized that 'his quiet masculine stubbornness and prosaic outlook on life is in striking contrast with her sparkle and brilliance. They make a fine team, and each complements the other.' The writer's comments could just as well have been applied to their real-life romance as well. Most of the nine films they did together reflected much of their personal rapport.

This first film of the series concerned the love–hate marriage of a sophisticated political columnist and a gruff sports writer. The scenario emphasized the feminist angle until, at the rewritten ending, she submitted to domesticity in order to keep the man she loved. Kate used strong language about the reactionary finale but it didn't offend Tracy's more conventional views on gender roles. Katharine had been brought up in an enlightened household to believe in women's rights, birth control and other advanced ideas, yet she willingly played a subordinate role in her relationship with Tracy. She did all the housework, the cooking, the shopping and the cleaning. When Ely Landau, the producer of *Long Day's Journey Into Night* (1962) in which Kate played Mary Tyrone, went to breakfast with the couple, he found it 'extraordinary to watch her with Spence. She was a totally different person. She turned really submissive – it's the only word I can use – and hardly opened her mouth, other than introducing us.'

Once, when they had guests, Kate picked up a log and threw it on the fire. Tracy reprimanded her sharply in front of everybody. She had intruded upon his territory. The guests were astonished to see she was not shamed but sat down beside him more loving than ever. He would call her names such as 'bag of bones' or 'Olive Oyl', and tell her to 'shut up for once', and she would accept it from him alone. Their good friend, the writer, Garson Kanin once asked Tracy why he always insisted on top billing in all their films. 'After all, she's the lady,' he chided. 'You're the man. Ladies first?' Tracy replied, 'This is a movie, Chowderhead, not a lifeboat.'

Nevertheless, although Hepburn called Tracy a 'sturdy oak buffeted by the wind – a throwback to an age of rugged heroism', she was the stronger of the two when it came to coping with day-to-day difficulties. She was the rock on which he could lean for support. It was not long after their first meeting that Kate was to come brutally into contact with a part of her lover that she would spend the best part of her time fighting. Halfway through shooting on *Woman Of The Year*, Tracy disappeared. Friends, and members of the crew who had worked with him before, knew that he had gone on one of his periodic binges. When he was not found at his usual drinking haunts, Kate went from bar to bar searching for him. She finally caught up with him, brought him home, fed him and sobered him up. On the set, for the rest of the picture, she brewed pots and pots of strong tea to serve him. Later she attempted to free him from his circle of drinking friends that included James Cagney, Pat O'Brien, Clark Gable and Lynne Overman. Kate made it her mission in life to save him from the ravages of alcohol.

Katharine Hepburn was strongly advised against entering into an affair with Tracy. There were so many good reasons why, if there had been a rational option, it should never have happened. Although he was only seven years Hepburn's senior, Tracy already had serious health problems at the age of forty-one when they met. Mainly due to excessive drinking, his liver and kidneys had been affected, and his heart was not too strong either. He was often moody, rude and short-tempered, and suffered periods of melancholia. Another negative aspect was the fact that, as a Catholic, he would never divorce his wife. This had not stopped him having affairs with other women. One of the longest had been with lovely Loretta Young, his co-star in *Man's Castle*. Kate's friends reckoned that if Tracy had not left his wife for Miss Young some years previously, he would never set up house with her. She would have to accept the terms of a clandestine relationship with all its pitfalls. But Kate was deeply in love with Tracy, and he saw her as his salvation – a woman who could share his work as well as his life, and accept him for what he was. By loving him she became a less self-absorbed person and also a better actress. 'He's my ideal,' Kate told Dick Cavett on TV in 1973. 'I mean what he does, I would really like to be able to do. And I learned a great deal from him.' At another time she stated that 'Much of what I know about acting I learned from Spencer Tracy.' As a doctor's daughter she was ideally suited to watch his health and drinking. She tried to keep him on the wagon, he tried to keep her feet on the ground. It is impossible to tell where their lives might have led had their paths not crossed, but hers would surely have been less happy and rich, and he might well have descended into the darkness.

Spencer Tracy had married former stage actress Louise Treadwell in 1923 when he was a struggling actor recently graduated from the American Academy of Dramatic Arts. Louise gave up her career when their son John was born a year later. At ten months old the baby was pronounced incurably deaf. When Spencer heard the news he went out and got drunk. Using sign language and other methods, Louise learnt to communicate with the child, who became almost wholly dependent on her. Tracy felt guilt and frustration at not being able to get through to his son. 'I wanted to help with the boy, but I was no good at it,' he later remarked. 'I had no patience, and it was amazing how much she had.' Louise not only had patience with John but with her erring husband. For nearly twenty years she supported him through thick and thin, bolstering him in his burgeoning career, and welcoming him home drunk and/or from the arms of another woman without recrimination. After Tracy became a major star around 1935 she was always by his side at important social functions. At the 1938 Academy Awards ceremony the tall, slim, dark and elegantly coiffed Mrs Spencer Tracy (as she was always referred to) went up to receive her husband's Oscar for *Captains Courageous*. (He was in hospital recuperating from a hernia operation.) 'I accept this on behalf of Spencer, Susie [their daughter, then aged five], Johnny and myself.' The applause which greeted her drowned any rumours of his liaison with Loretta Young. Ed Sullivan wrote in his column next day, 'Mrs Tracy stole the show. She is just the sort of person you expect Spencer Tracy's wife to be. Simple and unaffected.' In the same year that Tracy met Hepburn, Louise realized her dream of establishing the John Tracy Clinic for Deaf Children with herself as active president. It became one of the largest clinics of its kind in the world, where thousands of deaf children and their parents were helped at no cost. In 1956 she won the Save the Children's Foundation Award, and four universities bestowed honours on her. It was not easy for a man of conscience and ethics to walk out on a woman of Louise's qualities.

Although their marriage had long since deteriorated, strong ties continued between them. Throughout his life, which meant throughout his love affair with Hepburn, hardly a week went by without Tracy visiting Louise and his children at their home in Beverly Hills. From time to time photographs of the Tracy family together appeared in newspapers and magazines across the country in connection with Louise's work at the clinic. Despite John's deafness, he went to college and later married, and Susie became a fine professional photographer. Louise, knowing the marriage was over in all but name, never stood in the way of Kate and Spencer's relationship, and Kate was never jealous of Louise, a woman she admired. This mutual respect, born out of a shared love and concern for Tracy, would later result in the exceptional scene of the two women taking turns to sit by Spencer's bedside during his illnesses towards the end of his life.

Hepburn herself had once been married. She was an unknown stage actress of twenty-one and he was a handsome, wealthy, sophisticated New Englander called Ludlow Ogden Smith. They were married secretly in December 1928 by Kate's grandfather, an Episcopalian minister, in West Hartford, Connecticut. The marriage was kept so private that no public photos exist of the couple together. Shortly after she had become famous, when Kate was asked by reporters if she was married, she replied, 'I don't remember,' and to the query as to whether she had any children, she said, 'Yes, two white and three coloured.' Actually, she always claimed that marriage was not a natural state, and never expressed any desire to have children. From all accounts,

'Luddy' and Kate's marriage was closer to a platonic friendship than anything else. In 1981 Hepburn told Barbara Walters on television that 'I was self-centred. He was a nice man. I felt sorry for him ... I broke his heart, spent his money. ... ' They soon ceased to cohabit but remained good friends until his death in 1983. They were, in fact, divorced twice, in 1934 in Mexico and in 1942 in Connecticut, because 'Luddy' doubted the legality of the first decree and wanted to marry again. Kate had no intention of ever marrying again. In any case, after 1941, if she couldn't marry Tracy, she certainly wouldn't marry anyone else.

When Kate arrived in Hollywood in 1932 to make her film debut as John Barrymore's daughter in *A Bill Of Divorcement*, R.K.O. studio executives described her as looking 'like a cross between a horse and a monkey'. But she soon confounded everyone, helped somewhat by Hollywood's glamour treatment, by emerging, with her high cheek bones and natural looks, as a stunning beauty. She refused to give in to the studio's publicity demands by avoiding interviews and always wearing trousers off the set. As she prized her independence above all, Hepburn gave the impression of being aristocratic and snobby, gaining the nickname 'Katharine of Arrogance'. She always insisted that her private life was nobody's business but her own, yet her name was linked romantically with director John Ford, flamboyant producer Howard Hughes, and her agent Leland Hayward. Kate was smitten by the intelligent and dashing Hayward and, next to Tracy, it was her most serious involvement. However, he was never faithful to her or to his first wife. Curiously, the press stopped speculating about Kate's escorts and marriage prospects after her friendship with Tracy blossomed.

Following the success of the first Tracy–Hepburn pairing, M.G.M. quickly put them into another vehicle, *Keeper Of The Flame* (1942), a competent melodrama that made the mistake, as far as the public was concerned, of eliminating any love interest between the two. Another failure was *Sea Of Grass* (1947), also a drama. *Without Love* (1945), *State Of The Union* (1948) and, above all, *Adam's Rib* (1949) had them doing what they did best together, sparring affectionately and wittily in a bouncy battle of the sexes which underscored the stars' off-screen personalities. In *Adam's Rib* a home-movie sequence was very much modelled on how Kate and Spencer behaved 'at home'. If their real relationship was a clandestine one, they could at least relive it in fictional terms for all the world to see. They tried to work together as much as possible. Claudette Colbert was originally cast as the estranged wife of a presidential candidate in *State Of The Union*, but when she refused to work beyond 5 p.m. director Frank Capra sacked her. Capra phoned Tracy to tell him the bad news. Tracy, of course, knew someone who could fill the role. 'The bag of bones has been helping me rehearse. Kinda stops you, Frank, the way she reads the woman's part.'

During the halcyon days between 1942 and 1949, when they were paired six times, Tracy and Hepburn continued to live in separate homes. Kate ran both households in her capacity as Tracy's companion, secretary, nurse, cook and chauffeur. She even managed to stop his drinking. On weekends when they were not working she kept him as occupied as she could. They walked, swam, talked and painted. Everything in her life, including her choice of film roles, was dictated by Tracy's needs. On pictures in which she did not appear with him she would still drive him to the studio, remain with him on the set, drive him home and cook him a meal. In 1948, taking the opportunity of a stretch of time together in England, Tracy accepted the lead in *Edward, My Son*. During the shooting Tracy stayed with Laurence Olivier and Vivien Leigh at their huge thirteenth-century mansion, Notley Abbey, while Kate put up at Claridge's. He could not stay with her at the hotel, and they would not have felt at ease together at Notley. It was one of the coldest English winters for decades, and Spencer shivered in the cavernous rooms of the Abbey. He and Kate were glad to be able to film *Adam's Rib* next, in New York in the spring.

Adam's Rib (the original title *Man And Wife* was vetoed by the M.G.M. front office as being indiscreet) was written by Garson Kanin and his wife Ruth Gordon with Tracy and Hepburn in mind. It concerned a pair of lawyers, husband and wife, who find themselves on opposite sides in a court case. The film, heralded by the billboards as 'The Hilarious Answer To Who Wears The Pants!', helped give M.G.M. a financial shot in the arm. The *New York Times* wrote that Tracy's and Hepburn's 'perfect compatibility in comic capers is delightful to see. A line thrown away, a lifted eyebrow, a smile or a sharp, resounding slap on a tender part of the anatomy is as natural as breathing to them. Plainly, they took pleasure in playing this rambunctious spoof.' During the amiable atmosphere of shooting Kate lived at her house in Turtle Bay, not far from the city, while Spencer was ensconced at the Waldorf Towers.

For some months following *Adam's Rib* the couple looked for another script that would be right for both of them. When nothing suitable materialized, Tracy went into *Malaya*, an uninspiring action melodrama. Kate, meanwhile, was delighted to be able to take up an offer to play Rosalind in a Broadway production of *As You Like It*. She had never tackled Shakespeare before. 'I realize I'm putting my head on the line,' she said. 'But for me, the personal satisfaction justifies the risk.' She knew she was also taking a risk in leaving Tracy, who was finding it increasingly difficult to cope without her, for a nine-week pre-New York tour and then a longish run. While she was away he started drinking again, and phoned her about three times a day. As soon as *Malaya* was completed Tracy caught up with Hepburn in Cleveland where he promised to give up alcohol. But during the play's 145 performances on Broadway Spencer was seen reeling into and out of Kate's apartment night after night, until Hollywood beckoned him again.

With *As You Like It* behind her, Kate returned to California and Tracy. It was the early 1950s and Spence was being kept busy – and sober – making *Father Of The Bride*(1950) and its sequel, *Father's Little Dividend*, and was about to start *The People Against O'Hara* (1951), co-starring with his oldest buddy, Pat O'Brien. Kate decided to go off to the Dark Continent to make *The African Queen*, which was to be one of the greatest triumphs for her and her Oscar-winning co-star Humphrey Bogart. Despite the arduous location work in the Congo that left her ill and fatigued, Kate relished the challenge and the country. John Huston, the film's director, relates in his autobiography, 'I remember the many nights I sat with Kate on the top deck of the paddle boat and watched the eyes of the hippos in the water all around us. ... We talked about nothing and everything. But there was never any idea of romance – Spencer Tracy was the only man in Kate's life.' But if Tracy was the man in her life, she was the life in her man. Depressed by Kate's absence, he began drinking heavily again. After location shooting was completed, Hepburn and Bogart had to spend an extra six weeks filming in England. Tracy had arrived in London earlier to await her. There he met Joan Fontaine at a dinner party, and later phoned her to ask her out. Fontaine told Anne Edwards, Hepburn's biographer, that she declined the invitation out of respect for Kate, and also reminded Tracy that he was a married man. 'I can get a divorce whenever I want to,' he told her. 'But my wife and Kate like things just as they are.'

Back in America, Kate rolled up her sleeves and got to work on Tracy again, brewing endless cups of coffee, insisting he take cold showers, walks and swims every day. Now completely grey, Spencer looked much older than his fifty-one years, but Kate got him into reasonable shape again. She was greatly helped in her efforts by the fact that their good friends Garson Kanin and Ruth Gordon had another tailor-made script ready for them. *Pat And Mike* (1952) was a happy experience for both stars and for audiences everywhere. Filmed almost entirely at the Riviera Country Club in Pacific Palisades, it concerned the loving and bantering relationship between a sports promoter and an all-round sportswoman. A favourite line has Tracy saying, when he first claps eyes on Hepburn, 'Not much meat on her, but what there is is choice!'

In order to keep an eye on her loved one, Kate gave up work for a couple of years while Spencer made a potboiler, *Plymouth Adventure*, the charming Ruth Gordon memoir *The Actress*, a sturdy Western, *Broken Lance*, and *Bad Day At Black Rock*, an intriguing yarn stamped with Tracy's authority. Confident that he could be left alone once more, Kate took up the tempting offer to make *Summertime* for David Lean in Venice. But her absence again created a deep void for Tracy. He was set to make *Tribute To A Bad Man* opposite Grace Kelly. Just as he had sought female companionship from Joan Fontaine when Hepburn was in Africa, so he dated the cool blonde beauty. Kate heard rumours of a romance while she filmed in the muggy heat of the Italian summer of 1954. Tracy managed to visit her in Venice for a short period to reassure her that his dates with Kelly had been strictly business. The future Princess Grace backed away from Tracy and out of the project.

On her return from Venice Kate found it impossible to resist the offer of a tour of Australia in three Shakespearean plays, playing opposite her friend Robert Helpmann. Tracy took her acceptance of the tour as a personal affront. On the day she left for Australia in May 1955 he began to drink heavily. Shooting on *Tribute To A Bad Man* was due to begin on 1 June. Tracy arrived at the Colorado desert location six days late without any explanation for director Robert Wise. Two days later he disappeared again, causing panic among the crew. Calls were placed to Kate in Australia, who was in the midst of a demanding tour. After a week he turned up again, only to complain that he could not stand the altitude in the Rocky Mountains where much of the filming was to take place. Soon after, Tracy was fired and his twenty-one-year M.G.M. contract terminated. Thereafter, Tracy spent much of his time drowning his woes in alcohol and calling Kate in Australia, a situation not calculated to help her concentration in *The Taming Of The Shrew, Measure For Measure* and *The Merchant Of Venice*. She determined on her return never again to leave him for any length of time.

The gossip that Tracy would never be hired again in Hollywood was silenced when he was nominated for an Oscar in *Bad Day At Black Rock*. (Hepburn was nominated in the same year for *Summertime*.) But he was a very sick man from 1955 onwards. His liver had deteriorated, his heart and lungs were weak. Kate cut down her own smoking drastically in an effort to help him to stop, and she made sure he ate healthily, took exercise and lost weight. She nursed him, cheered him up and encouraged him to keep working. When Paramount signed him to do *The Mountain* (1956), she accompanied him to Chamonix in France for the location shooting. It was not the best choice of subject for Tracy, not only because he was unconvincing as a Swiss shepherd but also because the high altitude and the climbing required gave him breathing difficulties and put a strain on his heart and lungs. Kate managed to remain discreetly in the background during filming but hardly left his side when the day's work was done. When *The Mountain* was being completed at Paramount in Hollywood she accepted *The Rainmaker*, opposite Burt Lancaster, at the same time and at the same studio so they could be together as much as possible.

In the spring of 1956 Spencer and Kate flew to Cuba where he was to start filming *The Old Man And The Sea*. Leland Hayward, Hepburn's ex-agent and ex-lover, now a producer, had persuaded Tracy that he was the only man to play the ancient Mexican fisherman of Ernest Hemingway's novella. Tracy admired the book but didn't hit it off with the bullying author, who thought the actor

146

looked 'too rich and fat' for the role. There was tension, too, between Tracy and the director Fred Zinnemann. Unhappy about the film and under a strain, Spence began to tour the Havana bars, after which Kate would get him back to the rambling, fourteen-room villa where they were staying. She then decided that she would not allow her man to go through any more gruelling location shooting. When Zinnemann left the film the whole project was put on hold, and Tracy and Hepburn were able to return home. (It was later shot in a tank in Hollywood by John Sturges, and released in 1958.)

Happily, once back in the U.S.A. they were given an opportunity to make their first film together since *Pat And Mike* five years before. Since his dismissal from *Tribute To A Bad Man* Tracy had spoken of retiring permanently, and it needed all of Kate's cajoling to get him to work again. At first he was against making *The Desk Set* (1957), but he was somehow convinced that the picture could not be made without him, and he didn't want to deprive Kate of the pleasure of doing another film with him. A faint shadow of their previous confrontations, it would have been dire without the vibrant personalities of the incomparable duo. Working in Hollywood again, going for long walks, painting, reading and listening to music in Kate's company gave Tracy a new lease of life. They were closer to one another than ever but Hepburn was still an actress who needed to stretch herself.

Tracy seemed well enough again for her to decide to return to the stage in the summer of 1957 as Portia in *The Merchant Of Venice* and Beatrice in *Much Ado About Nothing* at the American Shakespeare Festival in Stratford, Connecticut. John Houseman, the artistic director of the festival, recalls in his book *Final Dress* how Kate kept talking about Tracy 'with a mingling of loyalty, tenderness and admiration' during the whole season. She also spoke continually of his imminent arrival from Los Angeles to see her. 'Finally,' Houseman writes, 'the great day came when Kate, with a young girl's enthusiasm, proclaimed that this time Spencer was really coming. His plane ticket was bought and all arrangements were made. On the evening of his arrival ... she drove off alone, in a state of high excitement, that she made no attempt to conceal, to Idlewild to meet him. Soon after she had left, there was a phone call from California. Somehow, on the way to Burbank, Spencer had got lost and missed his plane. He never did appear.'

For the next eighteen months Kate spent most of her time caring for Spencer. She even considered giving up her career completely. Uppermost in her mind was finding suitable scripts worthy of Tracy's great talent. She looked no further than *The Last Hurrah* (1958), the first picture of his final phase as the grand old man of movies. As an old-time Boston–Irish politician, Tracy gave one of his most subtle, witty and moving performances under the superb direction of his good friend John Ford, who had directed him in his very first picture, *Up The River*, in 1930. Kate was especially watchful on the set at Columbia as the supporting cast was almost exclusively made up of members of his old Wednesday night drinking circle – Pat O'Brien, James Gleason, Ed Brophy and Wallace Ford. She needn't have worried as by now they were all reformed.

When Kate signed to make *Suddenly Last Summer*, her first film for two years, she had thought the picture was to be made in Hollywood. However, in order to save production costs, producer Sam Spiegel decided to move the project to England. Kate was to find the entire enterprise distressing and distasteful. Firstly, she was distraught at being separated from Tracy, who was suffering from emphysema; secondly, she began to detest her role as the possessive, malevolent matriarch in Tennessee Williams' often ludicrous Gothic melodrama. Thirdly, she spent her time duelling with the director, Joseph L. Mankiewicz, over the interpretation and what she felt was his cruel behaviour towards an ailing and distressed Montgomery Clift, who was existing on a diet of codeine tablets washed down with brandy.

Kate was vastly relieved to return to America and her beloved Spencer. Apart from two months playing Cleopatra and Viola at the Shakespeare Festival in Connecticut in the summer of 1960, Kate seldom left his side. It was around this period that stories began to appear in print implying that Tracy and Hepburn were romantically involved, but little else was revealed. Insinuations were generally ignored, people preferring to see them as good companions of long standing. Until 1962 Tracy and his wife were still being photographed together. The deification of Mrs Spencer Tracy and her husband, nicknamed 'The Pope' by David Niven, prevented public gossip and censure. In January 1962 *Look* magazine revealed that Tracy had been an alcoholic, that he had been living separately from his wife for years and that he and

Hepburn were 'something more than frequent co-stars'. The article affected their lifestyle not at all. They still maintained two homes as a matter of principle, always stayed in separate hotel suites when travelling, and were almost never seen dining out together. Tracy continued to see his family regularly. In the early 1960s Kate and Spencer led a quiet life, entertaining only a few intimate friends. Tracy's physical condition improved, thanks to his abstention from cigarettes and alcohol.

In 1960 producer–director Stanley Kramer, who worshipped Spencer Tracy, offered him the meaty role of the defence lawyer in the notorious Tennessee 'monkey' trial of 1925 in *Inherit The Wind*. Kate had declined an offer to star on Broadway in Tennessee Williams' new play *The Night Of The Iguana* in order to be with her lover. She sat in a corner of the set knitting and peering over the rims of her spectacles from time to time to watch a scene. She was as protective of him as ever. So splendid was Tracy in the role that Kramer implored him to take the part of the American judge in *Judgment At Nuremberg*, to be filmed in the city of the title in 1961. Because of his admiration for Kramer, Tracy agreed, although he hated travelling. At the airport, as Kate and he were ready to leave, he suddenly had second thoughts. He hadn't been well for some weeks and wondered whether he could withstand the flight (he had difficulty breathing at high altitudes) and the location shooting. Kate took him aside for a few minutes, kissed him on the cheek and helped him to board the plane. When they arrived at Nuremberg airport a car was waiting to take them to their hotel. A few blocks away from the hotel Kate ordered the driver to stop. She got out, walked the rest of the way, entered the hotel by the service entrance, and went up to her suite – a common ruse to prevent photographers from snapping her in Spencer's company.

Soon after their return to America they were approached by producer Ely Landau to play James and Mary Tyrone in a low-budget film version of Eugene O'Neill's mammoth autobiographical play, *Long Day's Journey Into Night*. Kate readily accepted but Tracy said he would consider playing it for $500,000, which he knew to be an impossible demand. Perhaps it was his way of turning down a role he would have found too mentally and physically exhausting. Kate claimed that his performance would 'have pierced the sky'. A short while after the intense seven-week shooting of the film, something happened to make Kate retire from acting for five years. Tracy and Hepburn were on their way to a picnic one afternoon when Spencer suffered a heart attack. She gave him mouth-to-mouth resuscitation until the ambulance arrived. Once he was installed at the hospital, she called Mrs Tracy. It was then that each took turn to keep vigil by his bedside. Gradually Tracy recovered, and on his release Louise left him in Hepburn's loving care. By the spring of 1963 Tracy had recovered sufficiently to take top billing over a Who's Who of American comedians in Stanley Kramer's box-office hit *It's A Mad, Mad, Mad, Mad World*. But the heat of the Californian desert, where it was shot, weakened him greatly and he came home hardly able to walk.

For the next four years the couple were able to share each other's company without the interruption of work. Although Kate was offered roles to satisfy her artistically, she opted to remain beside the man she loved, helping extend his life as long as possible and be with him at the end. Yet they still kept up appearances by living apart, although in close proximity. On days when he visited Louise or she had errands to run, Kate would pack his lunch or dinner in a basket and leave it on his front doorstep. She was also careful to see that her fridge had a plentiful supply of milk, which Tracy drank, and the daily amount of beer his doctor permitted him. She made him exercise by going for bike rides, or flying kites on windy days.

In September 1965 Tracy was hospitalized again, this time with an inflamed prostate gland requiring surgery. Once again Kate and Louise took it in turns to be with him. All reports of his health were issued to the press by Mrs Tracy. The film colony was prepared for Tracy's imminent death, and spoke in admiring tones of both Hepburn's and his wife's devotion to him. Miraculously, Tracy improved, so much so that when he had been home for a little over a month Stanley Kramer proposed a script for a film in which Kate and Tracy could co-star again. The story of *Guess Who's Coming To Dinner?*, about a middle-class white couple coming to terms with their daughter's wish to marry a black man, appealed to Kate's liberal sentiments. Spencer left it to Kate to make the decision, and agreed to work on the picture without having read the script. It was good enough for him that Kate was enthusiastic, and that the film urged racial tolerance and understanding, a theme that was dear to his heart.

Kramer knew he was taking an enormous risk by hiring Tracy. The insurance company refused to cover the star, whose health they knew to be precarious. Therefore, Kramer personally accepted responsibility for any financial loss engendered should Tracy die during shooting. It was typical of Tracy that he was able to marshal his forces and use all his considerable skills and experience to fulfil his contract admirably. When he delivered the last line of the screenplay to Kate, 'If what they feel for each other is even half what we felt, then that is everything,' she was moved to genuine tears.

When *Guess Who's Coming To Dinner?* opened in December 1967 it carried an extra resonance. The critic of the New York *Morning Telegraph* wrote, 'Both of them are splendid, both of them are so beautifully matched ... that a lump rises in the throat on the realization that they will never appear together again,' and *The New Yorker* observed that 'when, at its climax, he turns to her and tells her what an old man remembers having loved, it is, for us who are permitted to overhear him, an experience that transcends the theatrical'. Both Tracy and Hepburn were nominated for Academy Awards. Louise, accompanied by her son and daughter, was present at the Oscar ceremony, hoping she would accept the posthumous award for her husband. Kate was in Nice filming *The Madwoman Of Chaillot* when the news came that she had won her second Oscar. 'Did Spencer win, too?' she asked. When told he did not, she replied, 'Well, that's O.K. I'm sure mine is for the two of us.'

In 1971 Garson Kanin's *Tracy And Hepburn – An Intimate Memoir* was published full of personally observed anecdotes that revealed much about their friendship. Although Louise was named beneficiary and executrix in his will, and was known as Mrs Spencer Tracy until her death in 1983, Hepburn was cast as Tracy's real widow. Kate told the London *Evening Standard*, 'I had twenty-five years of perfect companionship with this man among men.... Our films assumed that if the relationship between us was valid enough, the spontaneity would be there.... If people ask why our partnership was so successful, that's why – it was based on a natural and truthful completion of needs.'

LAURENCE OLIVIER
— AND —
VIVIEN LEIGH

H e was the crown prince of the great British theatre, she was Scarlett O'Hara.

The union of Laurence Olivier and Vivien Leigh is one of the most fabled love stories of the century. In the words of Sir Alexander Korda's son, Michael, 'By 1940 they were heralded as the most romantic couple in the world after the Duke of Windsor and Mrs Simpson.' A decade before the Bergman–Rossellini scandal shook Hollywood, Olivier and Leigh left their respective spouses and children and ran away together. They were in the grip of a passion and a mutual devotion which amounted to worship and which knew no boundaries, and they were almost literally unable to survive apart.

This truly golden couple triumphed over their difficulties, married, and settled to a life of public acclaim and private bliss that was the envy of their peers. But dark forces were conspiring against them – forces that would take them down a long road of anguish, suffering and destruction and make theirs, ultimately, one of the saddest tales that can be told.

On 5 November 1913, as the sun was setting over the majestic snow-capped peaks of Mount Everest, Mrs Ernest Hartley of Yorkshire, now resident in India, gave birth to a daughter. Her first and only child, christened Vivian Mary, was an exceptionally beautiful baby, whose heart-shaped face, beguiling mouth, ivory perfection of skin and mesmerizing green eyes would one day cause her to be labelled the most beautiful woman in the world. Gertrude Hartley, herself a pretty woman, was a devout Catholic, intent on educating her daughter in religious ways. Ernest was a good-looking and stylish man who had risen from fairly humble

153

origins to grow very prosperous in India. He had a great enthusiasm for amateur theatricals which revealed him as an unusually talented actor, and little Vivian made her first stage appearance at the age of three, reciting 'Little Bo-Peep' to an audience enchanted by her precocious command and fairy-tale looks.

The child's early years were spent in typically British colonial comfort. She was looked after by the traditional Indian ayah until the arrival of a governess to begin her schooling and, at the age of seven, protesting vociferously, she was packed off to England as a boarder at the Roehampton convent. Her initial unhappiness there was made bearable by the nuns allowing her to keep a kitten, the first in a long line of the cats she would cherish throughout her life. She soon settled down and became the most loved girl in the school. Vivian was a diligent student and displayed prodigious natural gifts for ballet, acting and music. Well before her teens she was developing the qualities which would characterize her adult life: as a friend she was generous, loyal and kind; as a companion warm and humorous; her flair for dress was exceptional, and her exquisite manners such that they would one day contribute to her fame as a gracious hostess. Perhaps her sense of orderliness and neatness was a little excessive in one so young and, from time to time, she would withdraw into reflective isolation. Her maturing beauty was now crowned with a head of rich dark hair to complement her perfect features.

In 1927 the Hartleys returned to England permanently. That summer they introduced Vivian to the delights of the Continent, touring France, Italy and Austria, and bringing the happy years at Roehampton to an end. In the autumn she entered a convent at the French seaside town of Dinard. After a year there perfecting her French, she was sent to another convent at San Remo to better her Italian, and was then allowed a spell at a small, exclusive school outside Paris which she adored. Her stay was cut short when Gertrude discovered that the girls used to sneak off, complete with make-up, to sample the delights of Paris, and she packed her daughter off to a school in Austria. During these European years Vivian had developed a fragile, wraith-like appearance, although she seemed in good health, and was given to odd bouts of moodiness. Gertrude put these down to age, Ernest to what he termed 'boy fever'. His daughter certainly attracted gaping admiration wherever she went, and was not unaware of the fascination of young men.

By 1931 Vivian Hartley was a lovely and accomplished seventeen-year-old whose schooling was complete and whose future had yet to be decided. That year was spent visiting the theatre and the opera, and attending a succession of balls and house parties. Throughout, Vivian was conscious of her desire to pursue the ambition she had held since childhood to be an actress. Finally she asked permission to study for the stage, and a delighted Ernest enrolled her at the Royal Academy of Dramatic Art in London. It was February 1932, and term would commence in May.

Meanwhile, at a smart ball in the West Country Vivian met a blond, good-looking barrister from London named Leigh Holman. At thirty-one he was the oldest bachelor she had encountered, which immediately invested him with a romantic aura in her inexperienced eyes. Holman was charming, decent, kind and reliable, but he was also a quiet, conservative man, uninterested in the theatre and preferring a cosy domestic life to a glittering social round. He could not then have realized how little he and Vivian had in common, and he courted her assiduously and with propriety. In his company she felt secure and at ease, and convinced herself that she was madly in love. At the age of nineteen the fun-loving, gregarious and stage-struck beauty became Mrs Leigh Holman in a full Roman Catholic ceremony at a fashionable church.

Throughout the courtship Vivian had attended RADA, but Leigh now persuaded her to give up and concentrate on her role as wife to a rising barrister. To Vivian this meant loneliness and boredom in a two-roomed flat. Weekends were livelier, with rounds of parties to attend and, after six months of marriage, she relished the excitement of being presented at Court. Her husband was unable to accompany her but, with her grace and beauty, she created a sensation and Queen Mary was heard to remark, 'What a lovely child!' After this glittering public exposure Vivian was determined to return to RADA and, using a series of wiles on Leigh, finally succeeded in doing so.

Shortly afterwards Vivian became pregnant but stayed on at the Academy until June, even though she was house hunting as well. Suzanne Holman was born on 12 October 1933. Her mother's diary noted, 'Had a baby – a girl.' This detachment was to remain, for, sadly, Vivian never expressed maternal instinct towards her daughter. She cared about her well-being in a perfunctory way and was neither hostile nor cruel, but conventional emotion was missing. In later years she suffered guilt over this. With the acquisition of a cook, a maid and a full-time nanny for the baby, there was little that Mrs Holman was called upon to do. She was just twenty-one years old, bored, restless and frustrated. She decided to pursue an acting career come what may.

At this time Laurence Olivier – as beautiful a man as Vivian was a woman – was already the leading matinée idol of the London stage. Endowed with every physical attribute an actor could wish for, he also had talent and unique skills which raised him far above the level of his contemporaries. He was marked out for greatness in the chosen profession with which he was utterly obsessed, and remains the most famous actor in the English language this century.

Olivier was born in Surrey on 22 May 1907, the second son of the Reverend Gerald Olivier, whose Huguenot ancestors had provided sons to the ministry since the seventeenth century. The Reverend Olivier was, outwardly at least, a forbidding man who inspired fear rather than affection in his young son. The boy worshipped his mother and suffered intensely on her death when he was only thirteen. Gerald had been involved in acting when a student at Oxford and he cut a dramatic figure in the pulpit, while his wife encouraged the young Laurence to act at school in an attempt to conquer his awkwardness. However, the boy had no clear line of ambition for the theatre, being attracted to the Navy and to farming, although he enjoyed acting. As a youngster there was little to indicate the fine physical specimen he would become in his twenties, and he has said of himself, 'I was born a weakling. As a child I was a shrimp, as a youth I was a weed.'

When Laurence was sixteen his elder brother went to India. The boy was bereft and asked his father how soon he could follow in Richard's footsteps. The Victorian minister replied, 'Don't be a fool, Kim [Olivier's family nickname], you're going on the stage.' The boy studied with an exceptional teacher, the renowned Elsie Fogerty, before commencing professional theatre work as a humble walk-on. He graduated to minor roles, and was engaged by the distinguished Birmingham Rep. for two years before landing a good role at the Royalty Theatre in London's West End. There he worked with a slim, dark, lovely young actress named Jill Esmond, with whom he fell in love. The young couple married in 1930, by which time Olivier's struggles were over. When Vivien Leigh entered theatre circles Larry, at twenty-eight, had worked in New York and Hollywood, and had a film contract with Alexander Korda. Women threw themselves at him on both sides of the Atlantic, but he was very happily married to Jill and impervious to the charms of others.

Vivian, meanwhile, had embarked on the difficult climb to recognition. Through the good offices of her friend Beryl Sampson she acquired an agent who insisted on a change of name. His own suggestion – 'April Morn' – was, thankfully, rejected by Vivian, and Beryl came up with Leigh. Then a theatre producer expressed a preference for an 'e' in her first name, and thus she became Vivien Leigh. The aspiring actress started with smallish roles in a handful of undistinguished films, but she was in her seventh heaven, getting up at dawn to go to the studios, a professional at last. Still her husband refused to take her seriously. He was indulgent, certain that she was merely 'going through a phase' and, besides, he enjoyed her new routine of staying at home in the evenings which was part of her film actress' discipline.

Vivien Leigh made her stage debut in 1935, creating a good impression in a play that didn't run. Then in May of that year she opened in the West End as the lead in *The Mask of Virtue* and became a star overnight. Driving home at four in the morning after the opening-night party, the taxi passed the Whitehall Theatre where Olivier's name was in lights. Later that day she confided to an astonished Beryl Sampson that, 'Someday I am going to marry Laurence Olivier.'

Vivien had first seen Olivier on stage the previous year and was completely hypnotized by him. It was not only his extra-ordinary talent that aroused her but his breathtaking physical presence, which had a powerful and unfamiliar effect on her. She loved her husband but in a comfortable, unexciting way, and had yet to be caught in the thrall of a grand passion. Olivier had become the object of her secret fantasies – she was certain that he alone would understand her ambitions, that the pinnacle of fulfilment would lie in acting with him. They had met in passing at the Savoy Grill where he was dining with his wife. It was no more than a 'How do you do' and a handshake but, from that moment on, Vivien decided she was in love with him, and persuaded herself that he was just as deeply in love with her. In truth, he was barely aware of her existence.

Vivien's new-found success changed all that. She went alone to a matinée of Olivier's *Romeo and Juliet* and went backstage to congratulate him on his performance. This time he was dazzled by her, but hid his reaction behind a mask of politeness. He did, however, invite her to lunch, ostensibly to discuss a new play she was to rehearse and, in a haze of excitement and expectancy, she made her way to their rendezvous at the fashionable Ivy restaurant. Larry was charming, witty and interesting beyond even *her* wildest dreams. He expounded on his passion for the classics, especially Shakespeare, and convinced her that her own professional future lay in that direction. She was completely carried away, but for one small cloud: they were not alone. At Olivier's invitation, John Gielgud was present.

With 1936 well under way, Vivien was now the proud possessor of a longed-for film contract with Alexander Korda, although she also worked in the theatre. The run of an open-air Shakespeare play at Regent's Park left her with serious flu. She recovered, but became painfully thin and suffered a worryingly persistent cough which didn't deter her from smoking very heavily. Korda, fond of Vivien and concerned about her, summoned her for a chat, during which Larry's name came up. Sensing her involvement, he reminded her that Larry was happily married and urged caution, but only a few days later he offered her the role of Lady Cynthia, one of the young lovers in *Fire Over England*. The man in the case was to be played by Olivier.

Vivien Leigh and Laurence Olivier were now thrown together daily. Each was drawn irresistibly to the other, and their on-screen romance swiftly became a reflection of what was happening to them off-screen. By the end of the fourteen-week schedule they were as inseparable as the realities of their lives would allow, realities which included the birth of Jill and Larry's son Tarquin, giving the actor an added burden of guilt and responsibility with which to wrestle. Exhausted at the end of filming, the couple each planned separate holidays, Vivien travelling with a friend, Oswald Frewen, as Leigh couldn't get away. On their way home Vivien and Oswald joined Jill and Larry in Capri for a few days. In the circumstances it was a surprisingly gay interlude, by the end of which Olivier had no doubt where his future lay.

Back in England Vivien and Larry became fully-fledged lovers. Leigh Holman seemed blissfully unaware of the liaison (although it was becoming common knowledge in acting circles), but Jill Esmond Olivier grew increasingly sensitive to the situation. As a Catholic Vivien didn't relish the idea of divorce; neither did she want to hurt Leigh. For a time she deluded herself that she couldn't possibly desert him or Suzanne, or allow Olivier to abandon Jill and Tarquin. Then in March 1937 the lovers co-starred for Korda in *Twenty-One Days*, prophetically playing a couple who run off together. Korda seemed happy to aid and abet his two beautiful stars, and gave them a week off to play Hamlet and Ophelia at Elsinore Castle.

Events moved rapidly. Together in Denmark, the couple knew they could never again be parted, no matter the price to be paid. Vivien wrote to Leigh and told him she could never return to him. He bore his heartbreak with fortitude, cherishing the hope that she would change her mind; Jill knew better and was shattered. Neither Vivien nor Larry found the decision easy, but there was no turning back. They bought a charming seventeenth-century cottage in Chelsea and moved in as man and wife in all but name, eagerly looking forward to the day when they would be free to marry. In the event, Leigh said he would not grant a divorce unless absolutely forced to do so, and Jill categorically refused Larry his. It was a deeply painful situation.

Professionally the starry pair were extremely busy and success-ful. In the summer of 1938 they enjoyed a glorious extended holiday in the South of France, during which they were asked to film *Wuthering Heights* for Goldwyn in Hollywood. It turned out that Vivien was wanted for the subsidiary role of Isabella and not, as she had hoped, Cathy, and she refused to do it. Reluctant to be parted from Vivien, Larry dithered for months before finally agreeing to play Heathcliff, and he left for Hollywood in November. Once there he fought with his co-star, Merle Oberon, was not well, and missed Vivien desperately. She, meanwhile, fell into depression and anxiety, smoked incessantly and suffered severe insomnia. By December she could bear it no longer and sailed for America.

On the night of 10 December 1938 the crew assembled to begin shooting the most famous Hollywood film of all time, *Gone With The Wind*. The first frames would capture the epic burning of Atlanta. It was all very exciting, except that there was no leading lady signed up. The by now desperate producer, David O. Selznick, had been searching for Scarlett O'Hara for two and a half years and, although every leading lady in Hollywood had begged for the part, he hadn't yet found what he wanted. Vivien Leigh longed to play Scarlett and had immersed herself in the novel, but Selznick was not interested in an unknown English girl to recreate the famous Southern belle. On that fateful December night, just as the glow of Atlanta's flames lit up the dark, Selznick's brother Myron arrived on the set with a pair of visitors whom he introduced with the words, 'Meet your Scarlett O'Hara.' David turned. There he beheld the living incarnation of Margaret Mitchell's tempestuous heroine, and a new Hollywood star was born.

Olivier and Leigh, the most 'English' of English actors, were now on the road to international stardom in the Hollywood tradition, living and working as part of the Tinsel Town community, but it was a difficult time. The need for absolute discretion was impressed upon them and, once again, they were forced to live apart and, worse, to practise a charade in order to save their reputations and careers from the fatal poison of scandal. With the outbreak of war they were concerned to evacuate their respective children, especially Tarquin who had been very ill with meningitis. This required a lot of money, so they were delighted when Korda asked them to star as Nelson and Emma in *Lady Hamilton* to be made in Hollywood. By now Leigh and Jill were relenting on the divorce front and freedom was in prospect. The strain of living in Hollywood was alleviated by a couple of Shakespearean theatre tours but during these Vivien began to display occasional outbursts of nervous edginess and ill-temper quite at odds with her usual personality. Olivier appeared not to notice – or perhaps he put it down to exhaustion – but neither was aware that these were early signs of the malady which would one day tear them apart.

At one minute past midnight of 30 August 1940 Laurence Olivier married Vivien Leigh in the living-room of friends in Santa Barbara. The long years of waiting were over and the newlyweds, if anything more in love than ever, enjoyed a brief honeymoon aboard actor Ronald Colman's yacht. Thereafter they had to sort out the problems regarding their children, and get on with filming *Lady Hamilton*. On 27 December, leaving Suzanne at school in Canada, cared for by Vivien's mother, and Tarquin in America with Jill, Mr and Mrs Laurence Olivier set sail for war-torn Britain.

The couple took a rambling house in the depths of the country and Larry joined the R.N.V.R. Vivien toured for six months in *The Doctor's Dilemma*, which took her through an icy and dismal winter in difficult conditions. By the time the play opened in London's West End she was once again pale, too thin, and coughing. A summer visit to entertain the troops in the North African sun didn't seem to improve her health. Home again, she became pregnant but nonetheless began filming Shaw's *Caesar And Cleopatra* opposite Claude Rains in July 1942. Six weeks later she was taken ill and lost the baby.

When the film was over Vivien became subject to acute depression although, outwardly, she maintained a vivacious front. As Anne Edwards, Miss Leigh's superb biographer explains it, Olivier '... was sympathetic but did not take Vivien's depression too seriously. Then, one night ... her mood suddenly shifted. Her voice changed, becoming strident, and when he tried to calm her she turned on him, first verbally and then physically. He was at a loss. For the first time she was a complete stranger to him.' The scene ended with Vivien in sobbing hysteria on the floor, after which she 'could not recall what she had done or said. It terrified them both, and immediately after she was child-like in her need to compensate. They were still totally in love and the effect on Olivier of such an attack was overwhelming.'

This distressing happening was the first of many such incidents which, over the years, grew more serious and prolonged. In fact, Vivien was a victim of severe manic depression that she could neither cure nor control though, helped by doctors and loving friends, she fought it bravely and managed to contain it for considerable periods of time.

In May 1945 Vivien opened in *The Skin Of Our Teeth* in London. She was alarmingly underweight and coughing badly but laughed it off, refused to see a doctor, and saw Larry off to entertain the troops in Germany. Meanwhile the Oliviers had bought a thirteenth-century house, Notley Abbey, in Buckinghamshire. Larry couldn't resist its historic connections and over-rode Vivien's protests at the immense amount of renovation needed to make the twenty-two roomed mansion warm and habitable.

While performing in her play, Vivien was caught up in supervising the restoration and decoration of Notley. It was all too much for her health. A doctor was called in and, without hesitation, diagnosed tuberculosis. The gods, it seemed, were intent on exacting a cruel price for the beauty, gifts and happiness they had hitherto bestowed.

A worried Olivier returned from Germany and installed Vivien at Notley, since she refused point blank to enter a sanatorium. She did not leave the house for nine months and spent the first four of those in bed, nevertheless immersing herself in the progress of the house and, notably, the gardens, in which she took a special interest. In the event Notley became a magic haven, much loved by its owners and the many guests who stayed there over the years. Hung with beautiful paintings and furnished in Vivien's exquisite taste, the graceful mansion embraced a succession of close friends such as Noel Coward, Katharine Hepburn, and other glittering figures. All this, of course, in between professional engagements both at home and abroad, including Hollywood, where Vivien won her second Oscar for her searing portrayal of the mad, anguished Blanche DuBois in *A Streetcar Named Desire*.

But under the surface life was a nightmare. Vivien's mental illness became more pronounced, and Olivier began to dread the onset of the attacks which he could sense in advance, and against which he was powerless to protect either of them. Still held together by deep love and the powerful memories of their passionate past, despair was also now a constant companion. The year 1956 was particularly traumatic. Olivier directed and starred in *The Prince And The Showgirl* with Marilyn Monroe, a fraught experience for all concerned. Meanwhile, after sixteen years of marriage, Vivien became pregnant again and seemed delighted. However, she miscarried and suffered a severe mental collapse – indeed, some of the symptoms seemed more like schizophrenia than manic depression as she abandoned her impeccable grooming, attempted to jump out of moving vehicles, became suicidal and abusive.

Throughout the years Larry had fought hard against his helplessness and anguish but, inevitably, hopelessness set in and he began to withdraw from this still ravishingly beautiful, warm, gracious woman who had for so long been his wife and his life. In 1957 he gave one of his greatest performances on stage in *The Entertainer*. He cast as his daughter a young actress from the north of England named Joan Plowright who, in every aspect, could not have been a more different woman or actress than

Vivien Leigh. Rumours of an affair began to circulate, and the press hounded the Oliviers. 'There is absolutely no question of divorce,' stated Vivien. 'Larry and I are very much in love.' But, alas, it was the beginning of the end. By 1958 husband and wife spent less and less time together; Olivier was in New York for most of 1959, and he and Vivien spent Christmas apart. They were also discussing selling their adored Notley.

On 19 May 1960, after receiving a long and moving letter from her husband, Vivien Leigh issued a statement to the press. 'Lady Olivier wishes to say that Sir Laurence has asked for a divorce in order to marry Miss Joan Plowright. She will naturally do whatever he wishes.' It was an agonizing severance for both of them.

Sir Laurence and the new Lady Olivier settled into contentment and raised the family he had never been able to have with his beloved Vivien. In due course he was made a peer of the realm and is Lord Olivier. He has had almost a dozen Oscar nominations and won the coveted award once for *Hamlet*. Now in his seventies, he has battled against severe physical illness with exemplary courage. He remains revered and admired on both sides of the Atlantic but, to this day, in his autobiographies and in live interviews, it is clear that the pain and the passion represented by Vivien Leigh have never been quite extinguished.

Vivien Leigh found comfort and some happiness with actor Jack Merivale, with whom she eventually lived and who cared for her with absolute devotion. She enjoyed periodic success on both stage and screen, notably in *The Roman Spring Of Mrs Stone*, and in a distinguished cameo role in her last Hollywood film, *Ship Of Fools*. In the early summer of 1967 she was taken desperately ill with tuberculosis, which had spread to both lungs. On 7 July, concerned for her health, Jack drove back from an out-of-town performance late at night but was relieved to find her sleeping peacefully. Fifteen minutes later he went to check again. She was lying face down on the floor. She had evidently got out of bed and, in so doing, her lungs had filled with fluid and drowned her. At the age of fifty-three the beautiful, capricious, fiery Scarlett O'Hara was dead.

In both London – with Laurence Olivier present – and Hollywood memorial services were held for this loved and tormented woman to which a galaxy of the most glittering stars of stage and screen came. In the words of Sir John Gielgud, 'She will not be forgotten, for her magic quality was unique.'

INGRID BERGMAN
— AND —
ROBERTO ROSSELLINI

I n the late morning of Sunday, 20 January 1957 a Constellation
aircraft landed at Idlewild Airport, New York. On board was
one of the most radiantly beautiful, most cherished, most
gifted and most famous stars the world has known.

Ingrid Bergman stepped on to the tarmac to be welcomed
by a small group of fans whose loyalty and devotion had with-
stood a storm of national outrage unleashed seven years previously by their idol. Now, filled with apprehension and choking
with conflicting emotions, this so-called scarlet woman was
returning to the land where she had vowed never to set foot
again. America had decided, not without hesitation, to forgive her
her sins.

And just what *were* these terrible crimes that she had committed? She had fallen in love with the Italian film director
Roberto Rossellini, and he with her. The power of the relationship persuaded her that she could no longer remain the wife of
Dr Petter Lindstrom, to whom she had been married for twelve
years and with whom she had had a daughter. After the news
broke that she had left Lindstrom, she was accused of betraying a
fine man and ruthlessly abandoning a defenceless child in order
to pursue the life of a shameless adulteress. When, in the course
of seeking a divorce that her husband was very slow to grant, she
bore a child to Rossellini out of wedlock, America was gripped
by a moralistic frenzy that knew no bounds.

The press heaped vituperation on Ingrid Bergman's head and
the Hollywood community which had adopted this foreigner now
gave her the cold shoulder. As if this were not sufficient, the
unfortunate woman was actually denounced from the floor of the

U.S. Senate. On 14 March 1950 Senator Edwin C. Johnson of Colorado delivered a vitriolic diatribe to the House, stating that Ingrid Bergman was responsible for 'an assault upon the institution of marriage'. Furthermore, he considered her to be 'one of the most powerful women on earth today – I regret to say, a powerful influence for evil... '. The senator suggested that her 'unnatural attitude toward her own little girl surely indicates a mental abnormality', and, having labelled her an alien guilty of moral terpitude (an offence against the law), claimed that she 'has deliberately exiled herself from a country which was so good to her'.

It is difficult today to read the accounts of the Bergman–Rossellini affair without a sense of sheer disbelief. It was certainly a major scandal but, to a disinterested observer, no more startling than many another private relationship that has been forced into the public limelight. Of course, in the restrictive moral climate of the time, to bear an illegitimate child was unacceptable, but that misfortune would not have occurred if Ingrid had been granted her divorce when she asked for it. As for deserting her husband for another man, as she herself reflected, divorces and remarriages in the film community were an everyday occurrence.

Why, then, was she forced to pay such a heavy price for following the dictates of her heart? Because she had become the American ideal. She stood for truth, integrity, moral decency and family values as no other Hollywood star before or since, and her worshipping public couldn't forgive her for betraying their faith in her superhuman perfection. As David Selznick remarked in the aftermath of events, 'We deliberately built her up as the normal, healthy, non-neurotic career woman devoid of scandal and with an idyllic home life. I guess that backfired later.'

Ingrid Bergman was born in Stockholm on 29 August 1915. Her German mother died when the little girl was three. From early childhood she was painfully shy and somewhat lonely and found her happiness in play-acting. Her Swedish father, a bohemian artist and photographer whom she worshipped, took her to the theatre where, enchanted by its make-believe world, she made up her mind to become an actress. That desire and, as it turned out, that *need* remained paramount for the rest of her life. The motherless child suffered another tragic blow when her adored and adoring, happy-go-lucky father died of cancer, leaving Ingrid orphaned at the age of twelve. Her spinster aunt Ellen came to take care of her but, unbelievably, Ellen herself died just six months later, in the arms of her terrified young niece.

The girl went to live with her Uncle Otto and Aunt Hulda, upright middle-class folk with several children of their own. They were kind to Ingrid and she attended an exclusive school in company with her cousins. During her school years her shyness was so painful that, on occasion, it induced unsightly physical allergies and she would blush and stammer on meeting people. Uncle Otto planned a conventional future for his niece, but Ingrid's determination to act was immovable and he finally agreed to allow her to audition for a place at Stockhom's hallowed Royal Dramatic Academy. Of course, the family never for a moment believed that so awkward and gauche a girl would succeed in her ambitions but, contrary to all expectations other than her own, Ingrid Bergman passed her audition and, in the autumn of 1933, aged eighteen, became a student at the Academy. She plunged into her new life with passionate dedication and, miraculously, her inhibitions and her psychological ailments disappeared. She was born to act, and her journey to success was swift.

Ingrid's private life, however, was somewhat restrained. In her splendid autobiography, while talking of her late teens, she wrote, 'I ... made an awful discovery. I was not popular at all with boys. I was too tall for them, or I was too gawky; I was too serious, I blushed, and I couldn't keep a conversation going ... there was only one thing to do. I pretended I disliked boys. I said, "I hate men...." ' I slipped away into my lonely play-acting and my obsession with the theatre.'

Shortly after her eighteenth birthday, a cousin persuaded Ingrid to make up the foursome for a night out. Her date was a young dentist named Petter Lindstrom, handsome, hardworking and, to a young, unschooled girl, the epitome of worldly sophistication. Petter was twenty-five years old and owned a car; he was a fine sportsman, an excellent dancer, and had a good sense of humour. He was highly intelligent and a model of old-fashioned moral virtues. Best of all, he seemed to take to his shy young partner, and within a few weeks they were seeing each other regularly. It was a considerable time before Ingrid and Petter realized that they had fallen in love and, although she quickly came to rely on his judgement, advice and opinions, they thought of themselves as just good friends.

Meanwhile, Ingrid reached the end of her first term at the Academy and determined to try and get some vacation work at the Swedish film studios. Her efforts brought consequences beyond anything she could have imagined: through a contact she was screen-tested by Gustav Molender, then Sweden's most famous film director and brother of the principal of the Dramatic Academy. The experienced Molender spotted the young girl's potential instantly and gave her a couple of small parts. The decisive moment came when Swedish Film offered her a contract, plunging her into confusion. 'How can you refuse such a contract?' she agonized in her diary. 'But I do not want to give up my theatrical career.' She took the problem to the other Molender at the theatre. He was furious, and in icy and dictatorial tones forbade her to give up her theatre training. That was quite the wrong approach – Ingrid Bergman may have been young and inexperienced, but she was also impulsive, hot-headed and stubborn as a mule. Stung by Olof Molender's attitude, she defiantly gave her services to his brother Gustav, thus beginning one of the greatest film careers of all time.

Her rise was meteoric and her fifth film, *Walpurgis Night*, attracted the notice of *Variety* in an era when foreign films were of little consequence in America. 'One of the better characterizations,' wrote *Variety*'s critic, 'is that of Ingrid Bergman. She is pretty, and capable of rating a Hollywood berth.' Prophetic words that would soon bring the young Swedish girl to Hollywood to follow in the footsteps of her revered compatriot Greta Garbo. On 16 November 1936, when Ingrid was twenty-one, the première of her sixth film was held. Co-starring with Sweden's most famous male star, Gösta Ekman, she played a young music teacher who falls in love with the father of her prize pupil. The film was called *Intermezzo* and Bergman was a sensation.

By now Ingrid was engaged to Petter Lindstrom, and the young couple married in July of the following year. They settled down happily, with Petter proving surprisingly adaptable to his actress wife's routine and needs. He was the rock on which she could lean at all times, and he encouraged her to accept an engagement with the well-known UFA Studio in Germany. While in Berlin she discovered she was pregnant but worked on undeterred. It was the terrifying rise of Nazism which, in the end, caused Ingrid to leave Germany without completing her contract.

In 1939 the Lindstrom's daughter Pia was born, and a subtitled version of *Intermezzo* was shown in New York and Hollywood. Again, the star was a sensation, and the Los Angeles *Daily News* suggested that 'Hollywood producers ought to form a pool to bring her out to this country.' Such measures proved unnecessary because one of Hollywood's most imaginative, exacting and powerful producers, David O. Selznick, sent for her. With war clouds gathering over Europe, Dr Lindstrom was only too happy to send his wife to the safety of America where he would eventually join her.

David Selznick had never encountered an actress remotely similar to Ingrid Bergman in attitude, and she had never conceived of a giant fantasy factory like Hollywood. Their first meeting was a make-or-break affair that took place in the Selznicks' kitchen (she was staying with them) at one in the morning. David's first words to his tall new import were, 'God! Take your shoes off,' and his next, 'Of course you realize your name's impossible.' It went on from there: ' ... your eyebrows are too thick and your teeth are no good, and there are lots of other things.... I'll take you to the make-up department in the morning and we'll see what they can do.... '

It was the first of many endurance tests for Ingrid Bergman, but her strength of character, which would seldom weaken, prevailed. She categorically refused to be put through any of the star-manufacturing machinery and suggested that, since Selznick obviously didn't want her as she was, perhaps he'd better not have her at all. It is a tribute to the producer that he capitulated on all counts, including keeping the publicists away, and gave strict orders that not a hair of Ingrid Bergman's head was to be touched. 'You are going to be the first "natural" actress,' he said to her. And she was.

Teamed with the British actor Leslie Howard, Ingrid commenced filming the American remake of *Intermezzo* and, by 1940, a new Hollywood star was born. The first couple of years were hard going – there were problems in finding suitable material for Ingrid and, aside from appearing in a Broadway play and making two unimportant films, she was marking time and grew restless and frustrated. Then her career snowballed. *Dr Jekyll And Mr Hyde* opposite Spencer Tracy in 1941 set her on the road; *Casablanca* with Humphrey Bogart the following year guaranteed her immortality; 1943 brought *For Whom The Bell Tolls*, paired with Gary Cooper; *Gaslight* with Charles Boyer in 1944 gave the actress her first Oscar; *Spellbound* in 1945 was her first for director Alfred Hitchcock and, also that year, she was nominated for an Oscar for her performance as a nun in one of the most commercially successful films of the entire decade, *The Bells Of St Mary's* with Bing Crosby. She was magically teamed with Cary Grant in Hitchcock's *Notorious* in 1946, and played *Joan Of Arc* in 1948, the year which turned out to be the most dramatically significant of her life.

In between this extraordinary run of films Bergman had made a couple of successful stage appearances and had grown in confidence as well as in popularity. Her husband was advancing in a career that took him from dentistry to become one of the world's most renowned brain surgeons. The couple had a comfortable home, a substantial income and a delightful and pretty little daughter. So much for surface appearances. Ingrid Bergman was no longer a happy woman. For all Petter's instrinsic virtues, his helpfulness to his wife had turned into a domination of her which curtailed her sense of independence. He had become critical of her and often made her look – and feel – foolish and inhibited. He was also puritanically frugal and she was unable to enjoy any of the frivolous luxuries that, with her income, she could easily have afforded. When, at last, she suggested divorce, Lindstrom was absolutely astounded and wouldn't even consider such a possibility, and the couple settled back into their familiar existence – solid, comfortable but, for Ingrid, emotionally unsatisfying.

Professionally, too, the star was unfulfilled. Her 1948 films were neither particularly good nor very successful; she felt under-used and back in a vacuum, looking for suitable scripts. Bergman was a woman driven all her life by a fundamental need to work, and to stretch and challange her abilities. Hollywood had been good to her and accepted her as one of its own and she had become a world-famous star, but there was a nagging awareness that she needed something more – something less superficial with which to engage her gifts.

Such was Ingrid's frame of mind when, one spring evening in 1948, she and her husband wandered into a small cinema to see an Italian film called *Rome – Open City*. It was a powerful example of the realistic cinema that had sprung from the ruins of war-torn Italy, and was as far removed from popular Hollywood entertainment in subject matter, approach and technique as anything could be. *Open City* was an emotionally shattering and impressive experience for cinemagoers, and nobody was more shattered or impressed by it than Ingrid Bergman. The film was the creation of an Italian genius whose name she had never heard: Roberto Rossellini. Who was he, this Rossellini of whom nobody seemed to know anything? The question haunted her and, a few months later while holidaying in New York, she stumbled on another of his films, *Paisan*, playing in an obscure little theatre, and excitedly went to see it. Again moved and impressed, she became obsessed with the desire to make a film with this man, but still the question persisted: who was he, and, more practically, how was she to find him?

Roberto Rossellini was born in Rome on 8 May 1906. His father was a handsome and accomplished architect, his mother a delightful and cultured woman and a devout Catholic. The family was extremely wealthy and kept a fashionable establishment on the Via Veneto, thronged with carriages and servants, and alive with parties. Rossellini senior was generous and extravagant to a fault and, with money no object, indulged his four children shamelessly. He died while still young, bequeathing his family a lifestyle which they enthusiastically continued to pursue even after they had more or less exhausted their father's fortune.

Roberto grew into a man of outstanding intellectual and artistic gifts, and developed an abundance of charm which seduced and hypnotized people into giving him what he needed, be it finance for a film project or credit at the local grocery store. His volatile temperament rejoiced in challenges and difficulties – he was, it is said, at his worst when life seemed to be proceeding too smoothly. Typically Italian in build and features, he was not a handsome man but women found him devastatingly attractive and he tended to return the compliment, falling in love with reckless passion and pursuing a relationship wholeheartedly until he considered it over. By the time Ingrid Bergman came into his orbit he had parted from his wife and was involved with the tempestuous and gifted Italian actress Anna Magnani. Warm, impulsive and generous, Roberto was also capricious, perverse, stubborn, irresponsible, and given to outbursts of Italianate rage. Nobody could have presented a greater contrast to the solid, Nordic reserve of Petter Lindstrom, or been more different from the ordered and conservative Americans with whom Ingrid was accustomed to associate.

Dear Mr Rossellini,
I saw your films *Open City* and *Paisan*, and enjoyed them very much. If you need a Swedish actress who speaks English very well, who has not forgotten her German, who is not very understandable in French, and who in Italian knows only 'ti amo', I am ready to come and make a film with you.

Ingrid Bergman

The writing of this famous letter began a chain of events as dramatic as any scenario for a romantic film. Ingrid wrote it a couple of days after seeing *Paisan* but had no idea where to send it. Some weeks later, stopped in a Hollywood street by an Italian autograph seeker, she asked the young man if he knew of Rossellini and was rewarded with the information that he worked at the Minerva film studios in Rome. In fact, Roberto was in the midst of a major row with Minerva and thus not on the premises. Unaware of this, Ingrid posted the letter, but the day it arrived the studios caught fire and burnt to the ground. There followed a minor miracle. The singed envelope was found among the ashes and a studio secretary contacted Rossellini who, totally uninterested, slammed the phone down on her. The girl persisted and finally sent the envelope by messenger to where a bewildered Rossellini, who didn't understand a word of English, gazed at it helplessly until his translator Liana Ferri came to the rescue.

Unusually for a director, Rossellini disliked actors and, for the most part, worked with people he pulled literally from the streets. He also seldom went to the cinema and, incredibly, the name Ingrid Bergman meant nothing to him. Liana Ferri did her best to explain until, at last, Roberto remembered that he had sought refuge in a cinema during a German bombing raid in the war and had been forced to watch the film three times. It was the Swedish version of *Intermezzo*. In a flash all Rossellini's ideas were overturned. Whether it was the appeal to his ego or his memory of Ingrid on the screen we shall never know, but he decided to rise to the challange of filming with this beautiful, international star.

The letter reached Roberto on his birthday and he replied with a florid cable that called it his 'most precious gift'. Shortly afterwards he wrote to 'Dear Mrs Bergman' expressing 'the extraordinary excitement which the mere prospect of having the possibility to work with you, procures me'. He went on to outline his ideas for a film – a bleak and tragic drama about a blonde Latvian war refugee who marries a poor Italian of savage passions and lives on a barren volcanic island. His description of the subject was long, complex and fascinating, and in the late summer of 1948 Bergman and Rossellini, conversing in French and with Petter in tow, met for the first time in Paris and discussed the project. Rossellini's working methods were, to say the least, unorthodox. Petter was cautious and sceptical; Ingrid was carried away on a cloud of euphoria.

Rossellini won the New York Critics award for *Open City*. He came to America in November 1948 to receive it and to pursue plans with Bergman, who had now involved herself in trying to raise American backing for the project. In January 1949 he returned to America and stayed with the Lindstroms in California. The mutual fascination that the fiery Italian and the cool Swede held for each other was undeniable, and their daily proximity sealed their fate. As Ingrid's biographer Alan Burgess phrases it, 'Ingrid's resolve to become a good wife and mother was now peeling away. She had known in her heart for a long time that if the right man came along and said the right words, she was ready and willing to go. In one short month, Roberto Rossellini did that. He did not equivocate. He did not seek justification. He did not say, 'We must think of Petter and Anna Magnani.' He said simply, 'Come away with me.'

The entry in Ingrid's diary for 20 March 1949 consisted of just one word, heavily underlined: Roma. Against Petter's wishes she was meeting Rossellini in Italy for a preliminary introduction to the country. The film (financed by Howard Hughes) was to be called *Stromboli*, the name of the island where it would be shot. It was a harsh, barren, inaccessible place, with no facilities for reasonable living let alone for film-making. The inhabitants were primitive, good-hearted and poverty-stricken peasants who lived surrounded by an often hostile sea and with Stromboli's threatening volcanic mountain looming over them. It was typical of Rossellini to choose such a difficult environment in the interests of truth and realism but, as yet, Ingrid had no idea of what awaited her there.

Meanwhile, the star arrived in the Eternal City as if in a dream. The sun shone, the waiting crowds gave her an ecstatic welcome. Roberto had arranged flowers, champagne, an abundance of presents, and a party of friends that included Federico Fellini. If the notorious *papparazzi*, the Italian news hounds with whom the couple would become all too depressingly familiar, were a little troublesome, they could not dent Ingrid's initial excitement and happiness. Roberto gave her a magic introduction to his country. After a few days in Rome which overwhelmed her, they set off in his sports car to the south, journeying through the villages of antiquity to the glittering Amalfi coast and the enchanting island of Capri. Ingrid was captivated by the light, the colour, the sounds and the spirit of Italy. And she was in love. Without reserve, with little thought for the consequences, she was floating in a fairy-tale land with her knight in armour. Roberto, in his turn, worshipped this woman, so challenging, so unlike any other he had known, and was determined to have her for his own. Neither realized the dangers that the profound differences in their temperaments would bring – blissfully unaware of the future, they lived the present to the full.

All too soon, reality intruded on perfect happiness, testing Bergman's iron endurance to its outer limits and beyond. Despair came daily to alternate with ecstasy but she didn't crack, for her devotion to Rossellini was absolute. However, Ingrid's conscience was deeply troubled. From Amalfi she wrote a letter, full of sorrow, to her husband telling him she had to make her life with Roberto. It was the beginning of a tormented and very protracted correspondence, for Petter could not face the truth. When, eventually, he did, he made conditions for divorce which dragged the unhappiness out interminably for all concerned. Worst of all, from Ingrid's point of view, she was to be kept away from her daughter for many years, thus carrying an additional burden of guilt.

Against this background the work on *Stromboli* commenced. As Ingrid and Roberto drove through Salerno he stopped the car and told her to wait while he found her a leading man. She was highly amused by the joke – until he returned, having placed a couple of raw Sicilian fishermen on the actors' payroll. That was Rossellini's method. On 4 April the director and his Hollywood star boarded a battered fishing schooner crammed with equipment and set sail for Stromboli. The first sight that met their eyes was the volcano towering two thousand feet above them, a rim of flame-coloured lava circling its smoking cone, and a carpet of ebony rock spilled down its side. The island was spectacular, primitive, hostile and remote.

Filming was a nightmare. Roberto's cast of amateurs slowed the proceedings drastically, as did periodic bad weather. Ingrid was exhausted by the physical demands on her, which included climbing the volcano, and donkeys had to be sent from the mainland. A member of the crew died from sulphur fumes. The schedule over-ran and the budget soared. R.K.O. Studios sent a succession of scriptwriters, production personnel and observers whose strictures were ignored by Rossellini. He lost his temper frequently; Ingrid was at the end of her tether. Their affair had become public knowledge and she was bombarded with letters from Hollywood dignitaries taking her to task and urging discretion. America was agog with the scandal. Ingrid tumbled from First Lady to Fallen Woman and even her films would soon be embargoed.

The unit finally left Stromboli on 2 August 1949. Incredibly, Rossellini and Bergman were still passionately, deeply in love. In Rome Ingrid – exhausted, conscience-stricken, depressed and shunned – could no longer ignore the fact that she was pregnant. She still had a husband and, worse, a ten-year-old daughter; the father of her child was a married Roman Catholic. It was not long before the international press got wind of the situation and blazoned it to the world. Ingrid Bergman's disgrace was complete. At Howard Hughes' request, gossip columnist Louella Parsons tried to soften matters with an article that began, 'Few women in history ... have made the sacrifice the Swedish star has made for love....' There was an element of truth in this extravagant claim – the impending birth of the baby was America's major news for almost a fortnight, relegating even Truman's announcement of the H-Bomb to an obscure paragraph.

Robertino Rossellini was born on 2 February 1950 in a Rome

hospital so besieged by the press that mother and child had to be smuggled home at four in the morning. A week later the baby's mother obtained a Mexican divorce by proxy. Roberto's divorce was through and the couple were, theoretically, now free to marry, but Italy didn't recognize Ingrid's divorce. The problem was solved with some ingenuity. Their great friend the Italian producer Marcello Girosi journeyed to Mexico together with a lawyer and the two men, standing in as bride and groom, exchanged the wedding vows on behalf of Ingrid and Roberto. At the same moment, in a moving and simple tribute to their commitment, the real couple knelt privately together in a tiny church near the Via Appia, silently joining themselves in marriage.

Mr and Mrs Roberto Rossellini settled down to married life – not that anything involving Roberto could be described as 'settled'. *Stromboli* proved a critical and financial failure when released, as did almost all the other films the couple made together. Artistically the pair were oil and water and could not be mixed. Domestically their relationship was passionate and loving, but also tempestuous and difficult, with Ingrid battling to understand and cope with her husband's mercurial temperament. (She had, at least, learned to speak Italian.) In 1952 Ingrid gave birth to twin girls, Isabella and Ingrid, and followed a routine of winters in their large apartment in Rome and summers in their house by the sea at Santa Marinella. Financially their lives were somewhat unstable, with Roberto's open-handedness bearing little relation to his income. It appeared that the Rossellinis had the happiness for which they had so dearly paid but, eventually, it became clear that their union was destroying their professional freedom and individual creativity without which neither could survive.

The year 1956 was a turning point. Roberto was invited to direct a stage play, *Tea and Sympathy*, with his wife starring, for the Théâtre de Paris and the couple were in Paris for discussions. Meanwhile, director Anatole Litvak was to make *Anastasia* (in England) for Twentieth Century-Fox and wanted Bergman for the title role. She had been exiled for seven years – would America accept it? Fox decided to take the gamble and it paid off. *Anastasia* was a huge success and won the star her second Oscar the following year. Hollywood and her public had signalled their forgiveness but Roberto was less than pleased. Jealous and possessive, he had not wanted her to go to England, and he also decided against directing the play. Ingrid, however, decided to go ahead and star in her Paris stage debut regardless, and thus their marriage entered a stormy phase in which a combination of separation and disagreement put a distance between them. Roberto went to make a film in India and rumours began to circulate that he was having an affair with his Indian leading lady Sonali Gupta. The rumours proved true, with Sonali leaving her husband and child for him just as Ingrid had done. Meanwhile, Ingrid began seeing the attractive Swedish theatre producer Lars Schmidt in Paris.

There was no dramatic upheaval. Indeed, there was no loss of affection. The Rossellinis, quite simply, had reached the end of the road as a married couple. They agreed lovingly and sadly that it would be in their best interests to part. It is a testament to their respect and admiration for one another, and to the strength of the deep devotion and passion they had once shared, that they remained caring, loving friends until Roberto's death in 1977.

Ingrid Bergman married Lars Schmidt, but they divorced sixteen years later, largely as a result of the constant separations caused by her career. She died in 1982 after an awesomely courageous battle against cancer, having regained her position as one of the world's best-loved stars, and having been acclaimed for her finest work in the second half of her extraordinary life.

MARY PICKFORD
— AND —
DOUGLAS FAIRBANKS

When it was announced by the press in banner headlines on 30 March 1920 that 'America's Sweetheart', Mary Pickford, had married Douglas Fairbanks, the screen's favourite All-American boy, the public at large threw their hats in the air. The clean-living athletic hero had won the hand of their beloved Little Mary. It was not more than eighteen months since the Great War, and there was a longing for glamour, escape and romance. Motion pictures provided them, and Mary and Doug's love story was equal to anything on film. 'The most popular couple the world has known' were photographed together ready to embark on their honeymoon, his muscular build, handsome bronzed features and flashing smile contrasting with her petite figure, peaches-and-cream complexion, hazel eyes and celebrated blonde curls framing her doll-like face. They were taken to the public's hearts as the epitome of romantic love.

Once the newlyweds were installed in their eleven-room suite at the Ritz-Carlton in New York, *en route* to Europe, news of their whereabouts spread through the city. Fans began to gather at the entrance of the hotel on Madison Avenue until the entire block was filled with people. Police had to clear the way for them to reach the S.S. *Lapland*, bound for Southampton. When the ship docked in England two planes swooped overhead dropping messages of welcome and bunches of flowers. At Waterloo station the couple were beseiged by adulatory Londoners. Outside the Ritz Hotel where they stayed crowds waited all night to catch a glimpse of their idols arriving or leaving. The honeymooning stars could go nowhere without being asked for their autographs or being showered with presents. When they attended the annual Theatrical

Garden Party in the grounds of Chelsea Hospital, a multitude of admirers pressed towards them so that Doug had to hoist his frightened wife on to his broad shoulders and carry her to safety.

Scenes like these were repeated all over the Continent. Because the silent cinema had no language barriers, Doug and Mary were admired and adored around the world. Only in Germany, where their films had not been shown during the war, were they ignored. Doug asked Mary, 'How do you feel about it? Do you like being left alone?' 'I definitely do not, Douglas,' she replied. 'Let's go some place where we are known. I've had enough obscurity for a lifetime.' In Paris they literally stopped the traffic on a visit to Les Halles one morning. A crowd of fans headed by sports champions Jack Dempsey and Babe Ruth greeted them on their return to New York, and a motorcycle police escort led their limousine, bedecked with American flags, through the multitude-lined streets. From there the uncrowned King and Queen of Hollywood returned to their palace, famously named Pickfair, in Beverly Hills, where they began their long reign.

Although Douglas Fairbanks was ten years Mary Pickford's senior, she had been in pictures for six years and at the age of twenty-two was earning $100,000 a year when he arrived to take the silent cinema – and Mary – by storm in 1915. She was born Gladys Smith in Toronto on 8 April 1893 of a poor working-class family. She never forgot her humble beginnings and, years later, as the hostess with the mostest in Hollywood, said to herself in her bedroom at Pickfair, 'Imagine you, Gladys Smith, of Toronto, Canada, with the Queen of Siam in your bathtub.' After her labourer father was killed in a work accident, the five-year-old child found herself the breadwinner of her family when her formidable mother Charlotte put her on the stage. Billed as 'Baby Gladys', she toured with various road companies. At fourteen, David Belasco, Broadway's most successful producer and playwright, gave her a leading role in *The Warrens Of Virginia*, and changed her name to Mary Pickford.

At the same time, twenty-four-year-old Douglas Fairbanks also had his name in lights outside a Broadway theatre. He was born Douglas Elton Ulman in Denver, Colorado on 23 May 1883. His father, a prominent Jewish lawyer, left home when Doug was five, and his mother Ella reverted to the surname of her first husband, the late John Fairbanks. From the age of sixteen Doug appeared on the New York stage, soon making a name for himself as a juvenile. In 1907, the year of Mary's Broadway debut, he was appearing in a play called *The Pit*. In the audience was a young society girl called Beth Sully who arranged a meeting with the actor. She fell in love with him and Douglas, always a bit of a snob, was dazzled by her wealth and social position. He was also very fond of the pretty, rather plump girl, who resembled his mother – fond enough for him to give up the stage to please her father Daniel J. Sully, known as 'The Cotton King', and take a job selling soap in one of Sully's companies after marrying Beth. But within two months he was back on Broadway, and his father-in-law became resigned to having an actor in the family.

After *The Warrens of Virginia* ended a sixteen-month run, Mary decided to try her luck in motion pictures. Pickford's first screen appearance was in *Her First Biscuits* (1909), a seven-minute comedy directed by the up-and-coming D. W. Griffith at Biograph Studios in New York. She made a further seventy-eight short films (mostly directed by Griffith) in her three years at Biograph. Although players were still uncredited at the time, Mary soon gained public recognition as 'The Girl With The Golden Curls'. In the company was a dark, handsome Irishman named Owen Moore. He taught her how to make love on screen, and they appeared in over a dozen pictures together. Charlotte disliked Owen and forbade Mary to see him outside work, but the usually dutiful sixteen-year-old daughter started to see Owen secretly. After Charlotte was told that they had married on 7 January 1911, she 'cried for three days and nights', according to Mary.

The marriage was not a happy one. It was the classic case, demonstrated in films like *A Star Is Born* (in which, in the 1937 version, Owen Moore himself had a small role) where a husband finds his masculine pride threatened by the fact that his wife earns more money and is more famous than he. 'It was, in many ways, an impossible position for any man,' Mary recalled. 'Those blonde curls hanging down my back must have been a grotesque and daily reminder that a child headed the family.' But Mary was no child when it came to business matters. In 1912 she had negotiated a $500-a-week salary at Adolph Zukor's Famous Players, which was doubled periodically. But it was not only Owen's resentment of his wife's superior financial and social status that caused a rift. He never got on with her family and he was a heavy drinker, an affliction that was aggravated by his married life. Mary took refuge with her mother a few months before the meeting that was to change her life.

Douglas Fairbanks was unimpressed by the few films he had seen and was inclined, like many stage actors at the time, to look down on the medium. He was quite content to be packing them in on Broadway to see him in comedy-melodramas in which he established the character of the smiling athletic hero that would soon make him a film legend. His reservations about motion pictures were dispelled after the first of several visits to see D. W. Griffith's masterpiece *The Birth Of A Nation*. In June 1915 Douglas, Beth and six-year-old Douglas Jr went to California where Fairbanks accepted an offer to play the lead in a film. He was thirty-two years old and was taking a gamble by giving up the New York stage. He needn't have worried because his first film, *The Lamb*, supervised by Griffith, was a hit and he became a star overnight.

Back in New York in the autumn of 1915 Douglas and Beth were invited to a Sunday afternoon party at the country home of musical-comedy star Elsie Janis. On the way, Doug was waved down by a chauffeur-driven limousine. The chauffeur was lost and needed directions. Doug took off his hat and introduced himself to the occupants of the car, who happened to be Owen Moore and his wife Mary Pickford, temporarily together again for the social occasion. Later that afternoon Doug, Elsie and Mary went for a walk around the estate. Beth had preferred to remain at the house, and Owen was propping up the bar. When the three of them came to a swiftly moving river, Doug and his hostess crossed on stepping-stones. However, Mary, halfway across, had difficulty keeping her balance, and was afraid to go on. Doug, living up to his heroic persona, ran back along the stones, swept Mary up in his arms and carried her to the bank. It was just the sort of scene that, in the plays and films they had enacted, always led to romance. On the walk back to the house there was a quiet intimacy between them. Mary's interest in him was aroused, although she thought him rather a show-off. He could not help but compare the tiny, fragile-looking young woman, the idol of millions, with his largish, bossy wife.

Fate threw Pickford and Fairbanks together again a few days later at a dinner-dance at the Algonquin Hotel. They sat together, chatting enthusiastically about films. Beth had no objection to their talking about a subject to which she was rather indifferent, and Owen was away filming in California. The two stars spoke of their admiration for *The Birth Of A Nation* and for each other's work. Mary had seen Fairbanks in *Gentleman Of Leisure* on Broadway four years earlier and had been impressed. She complimented him on his performance in *The Lamb*, to which he replied with uncharacteristic modesty, 'Beginner's luck.' He, in turn, told her he considered her Charlie Chaplin's equal in pantomime. They relished the mutual praise, particularly as both Owen and Beth were in the habit of belittling their work. Mary wrote later that she had 'hugged the echo of his words for days'. Their conversation was continued a little over a week later at the Screen Club Ball at the Hotel Astor. This time they found a common interest in sport. Doug was pleasantly surprised to learn that Mary shared his love of riding, had flown in an airplane (a rare thing in 1915), and had driven an automobile on a racetrack at a speed of fifty-six miles per hour.

It was not long before Doug was inviting Mary and her mother to tea at his mother's apartment. Neither Charlotte nor Ella got on with the respective spouses of their children and subtly encouraged what they recognized was happening between Doug and Mary. While the two mothers became acquainted, their offspring sat together in an alcove like teenagers in love. Mary was enthralled by the tales of his adventures and travels. He was a good listener too. The screen-writer Frances Marion wrote, 'You never thought of Mary as being sexy until Doug. He was so physical... Another thing, he'd listen to Mary. He treated her like an intelligent person. Any woman goes for that.' Although they were both enormously popular and extremely well paid for what they enjoyed doing, they were uneasy in their marriages. Outside her family Mary had few friends and was often depressed and lonely. Doug's wife had little feeling for the film industry, although she handled most of his business dealings. He also found it difficult relating to his young son. It was only when Douglas Fairbanks Jr was in his twenties that any affection was shown between them.

In 1916, while their careers were progressing by leaps and bounds (in Doug's case), and by hops and skips (in Mary's), they attempted to suppress their feelings for one another. Mary, a

Catholic, had the greater struggle. In her religion there was no divorce or adultery. At the end of the year Ella Fairbanks died in New York of pneumonia, aged seventy. Doug was dry-eyed and unemotional at the funeral. Afterwards he phoned Mary, who was in New York, and asked her to meet him. She collected him in her curtained limousine and they went for a drive in Central Park. Doug talked about his mother, and began to weep for the first time since her death. Then they noticed that the clock on the dashboard had stopped at exactly the hour of Ella's death. Doug and Mary, who were both superstitious, thereafter always made promises to each other 'by the clock'. It was then that they realized there was no turning back from their love for one another. However, each was aware that public knowledge of their affair could jeopardize their careers. As Mary said, 'We were falling in love and it was too late to save the loneliness and heartache and to escape the cruel spotlight of publicity. We fought it, we ran away from it.... The roles we portrayed on the screen had built up a special picture of Douglas and me in the world's eyes. Both of us, I perhaps more acutely than Douglas, felt this obligation to the public.'

The romance continued on its bitter-sweet way throughout the spring and summer of 1917. They were happy enough to be in each other's company during their frequent secret assignations and tried not to think of the future. Often, disguised behind motorists' caps and goggles, they would drive out in a Model T to a wild and desolate spot in the Santa Monica mountains. Far away from prying eyes, they would take off their masks and fall into each other's arms. Mary had tried to make a last go of it with Owen, but he continued to get drunk and abuse her. Beth, who spent a great deal of time in New York, seemed blissfully ignorant of the situation. Meanwhile, the protagonists of the drama threw themselves into work, Douglas as the All-American optimist in comedy-adventures and social satires like *A Modern Musketeer*, and Mary doing her sunny child impersonations in *The Poor Little Rich Girl* and *Rebecca Of Sunnybrook Farm*.

After America entered the war Pickford, along with Fairbanks, Chaplin, cowboy star William S. Hart and comedy actress Marie Dressler were asked to tour the country to promote and sell Liberty Bonds in early 1918. During the tour adulation of the stars reached its highest pitch. Chaplin did his famous walk,

Doug did somersaults, and Mary shook her curls and shouted, 'I am only five feet tall and I weigh one hundred pounds, but every inch of me and every ounce of me is fighting American.'

The tour was not only significant in that it got Pickford, Fairbanks and Chaplin thinking of forming their own independent film distribution company (which became United Artists in January 1919), but it also led to Doug's divorce. When the tour reached New York Beth, who was living at the Algonquin with Douglas Jr, expected her husband to stay with her for a few days. Instead, having just left the woman he loved, Doug could not face his wife, and moved into the Sherry-Netherland Hotel. This act at last convinced Beth that the rumours she had been hearing concerning Doug and Mary had been true. She told the press to announce that she and Doug had agreed to a separation, and named Mary Pickford as the other woman. When reporters caught up with Doug and Mary in different places, each issued flat denials but in spite of protestations, Beth filed for divorce. It was granted in March 1919, and Doug settled half a million dollars on his wife and nine-year-old son.

Now free to marry Mary, Doug began a constant battle to undermine her resistance to divorcing Owen, a step she was reluctant to take, although the marriage had broken down irretrievably. Now thirty-six, Doug wanted to set up home with Mary as man and wife. It was four years since they had fallen in love and they were still meeting secretly away from the studios. She continued to worry about what a divorce would do to her 'Little Mary' image. The situation came to a head in 1920 while he was on location in the west making *The Mollycoddle* and she was in Chicago publicizing *Pollyanna*. He called her and explained that he was tired of waiting for her to get a divorce; unless she made a decision immediately, he would disappear from her life. In tears, she told Charlotte what Doug had said. 'Remember, Mary, you're America's Sweetheart,' said her mother. 'I only want to be one man's sweetheart and I'm not going to let him go,' she cried. Finally, Mary Pickford gained a divorce from Owen Moore in Nevada on 1 March 1920, but not before Owen had brandished a gun threatening to kill 'that climbing monkey' Fairbanks, and demanded a large settlement.

A little over three weeks later one of Hollywood's legendary marriages took place at a Baptist minister's home in Glendale,

California. Mary wore a simple white tulle dress, Doug's brother Robert was best man, and Marjorie Daw, Fairbanks' frequent co-star, was the bridesmaid. After the small, private ceremony the bride and groom returned to Doug's house in Beverly Hills. 'The house is yours, Mary,' he said. 'It's my wedding present to you.' Some time before Mary's divorce Doug had rented a thirty-six room house in Summit Drive, Beverly Hills, one of the few residences in an area covered mostly by beanfields. He liked the site as it was isolated and only seven miles from the sea. He thought of buying the house, but Mary considered it 'too big and too brown'. Therefore he bought a hunting lodge in eighteen acres, and converted it into an attractive Tudor-style mansion with a view of the Pacific Ocean. Pickfair has since passed into Hollywood mythology as the symbol of Filmland at its most glamorous, the pinnacle of social life, the place where every visitor or resident of Los Angeles longed to be invited. Its name also linked Mary Pickford to Douglas Fairbanks for ever.

In 1922 the rapidly-growing film colony was shaken by the Fatty Arbuckle and William Desmond Taylor scandals involving murder, sex, drugs and booze. Doug and Mary set out to change the bad reputation that film people acquired. Their guest lists usually included some nobility, politicians, artists and sportsmen. Albert Einstein, Lord and Lady Mountbatten, the Duke and Duchess of Alba, tennis champion Bill Tilden and violinist Jascha Heifetz would rub shoulders there. Although the dinners were lavish, no alcohol was served and parties broke up around ten o'clock after hot chocolate had been served. Gloria Swanson remembered the Pickfair parties as 'deadly'. Nevertheless, the number of luminaries present was enough to dazzle anybody. The house had a plentiful supply of spacious rooms; the living-room, dominated by a huge fireplace, was imposing; the kitchen was modern, and the dining-room table was set for fifteen every night in case of visitors. There was a swimming pool complete with sand beach, and stables for horses. The rooms were filled with treasures from all over the world: a one-hundred-and-two-piece porcelain tea service that Napoleon had given Josephine in 1807; silk tapestries; jade and ivory *objets d'art* from the East; priceless paintings. Guests ate off a gold dinner service while a footman stood behind each chair. They had fourteeen live-in servants, including an impressive butler. Doug and Mary were the first in Hollywod to have a private screening room in their home, and unreleased films were often shown after dinner. Despite the lack of alcohol, Doug had installed an authentic mahogany California Gold Rush saloon bar. 'This is a happy house,' Mary stated in 1923. 'This is a house that has never heard a cross word.'

Pickford and Fairbanks became the ideal representatives of the film industry. They laid cornerstones, reviewed parades and opened fairs. They were among the thirty-six charter members of the Academy of Motion Pictures, Arts and Sciences, and Doug was its first president. On their various trips abroad they found their popularity unabated. In the summer of 1924 they were presented to the Kings and Queens of Norway and Spain. Two years later they were mobbed in Warsaw, Prague and Moscow. They even appeared in a cameo in the Russian film entitled *The Kiss Of Mary Pickford*. Benito Mussolini exchanged autographs with them.

For the first eight years of their marriage Doug and Mary were inseparable. If he was making a film on location, for example, she would travel there after work, stay the night with him, get up at dawn and drive back to Hollywood. It was a tradition that Doug always sat on her left at the dinner table. When they were invited out Mary would call the hostess in advance to request that she arrange the seating that way. 'I didn't even go to downtown Beverly Hills without first telling him where I was going and promising to call from there or having him call me,' recalled Mary. She referred to Doug as her 'companion, teacher, helpmate and guide'. He gave Mary credit for his success. 'Mary made me go out and get bigger stories, better cameramen and directors,' he claimed. Fairbanks' reputation was enhanced by superb productions such as *The Three Musketeers*, *Robin Hood* and *The Thief Of Bagdad*. For Mary, however, no matter how much she struggled to get away from her little girl persona, attempting more sophisticated roles like *Rosita* (1923) and *Dorothy Vernon of Haddon Hall* (1924), the public forced her back into curls and short dresses. A fan wrote to *Photoplay* in 1925, begging Mary not to abandon the 'illusion that there are such little girls and that we have one before us....'

In October 1927 motion picture history was made when *The Jazz Singer*, the first sound feature, was shown to the public. Fairbanks and Pickford had made their names in silent films, and felt threatened by talking pictures. Doug made a token gesture towards the new technique by introducing a spoken prologue and epilogue into *The Iron Mask* (1929). Mary decided to take a big gamble by making an all-talking film. She bravely set out to create a new screen image for *Coquette* (1929), and photos of her having her curls cut off and her hair bobbed were published around the world. The risk paid off when Mary became the second woman to win a Best Actress Oscar.

A short time later the couple finally agreed to appear in a picture together, something the public had been demanding for years. As the Burtons would do some four decades later, they chose *The Taming Of The Shrew* (1929). It proved to be not only a battleground for Petruchio and Katharina but for Doug and Mary as well. The differences in their attitudes to film-making became plain during the shooting. Doug would arrive late each morning after having done his daily exercises and sunbathing. Mary liked starting early. When Doug did arrive, he didn't know his lines and had to have them written on large blackboards. They also became acting rivals for the first time. Doug would criticize his wife in front of the crew, saying that he had played Shakespeare before and she had not. 'My confidence was completely shattered, and I was never again at ease before the camera or microphone,' Mary remembered. The film pleased neither their fans, nor lovers of Shakespeare, and was a contributing factor to the break-up of their marriage.

It is difficult to pinpoint an exact moment or reason for the first cracks which appeared in the apparently sturdy edifice of their relationship. Firstly, the basic differences and flaws in their characters became more obvious as they grew older. 'They separated on taste long before a third person came into it,' remarked Lillian Gish. 'Douglas liked to travel, Mary liked to stay at home. Douglas wanted to live in the world, she wanted to withdraw from it.' In 1929, on the last of their several trips abroad that year, Mary spent much of the time in her hotel, while Doug went out to meet the population. In the Far East she found the exotic food made her ill, so when Doug was out eating with the natives or playing golf she was left alone with an upset stomach. Other differences emphasized a rift. Mary had a better head for business than Douglas and would often clamp down on some of his extravagances. He was naturally prodigal, she was naturally frugal. His egotism was renowned, she was more modest. Fairbanks was known to possess forty suits, one of which he would select each morning, with the right tie and socks, to go to the studio. He was also obsessed with preserving his youth and was instrumental in starting the fad for suntanning among American men. Mary would always protect her china-doll complexion from the sun.

Fairbanks was also a very jealous person. Once when Rudolph Valentino arrived at Pickfair, Doug made it clear to him that he was not welcome. He reckoned that if every woman was said to fall under the Great Lover's spell, then Mary could not possibly be immune. On another occasion Doug turned up on the set of Mary's last silent film, *My Best Girl* (1927), in which she received her first screen kiss from handsome twenty-two-year-old Charles 'Buddy' Rogers. Doug left abruptly, later admitting to his brother Robert that, 'It's more than jealousy. I suddenly felt afraid.' However, in this case he had grounds. Rogers had a crush on Mary, and she was flattered by the attentions paid to her by a man eleven years her junior. 'In the early years of our marriage,' Mary wrote, 'I adjusted to his jealousy fairly well, but it later became a great trial to me. Douglas was even jealous of my mother.'

Mary's extreme closeness to her mother was a major irritant to Doug. When Charlotte died of breast cancer in March 1928 Mary became hysterical and hit her husband about the face, accusing him of hating her mother. Subsequently, Mary began to dabble in spiritualism to try and make contact with her dead mother. It was around this time that Mary became a secret drinker. Ever since Doug's father, an alcoholic, had deserted his wife and young children, Doug had detested liquor. In fact, when he was twelve his mother made him swear never to touch a drink until he was forty. Although Mary would keep alcohol in bottles labelled medicine or toilet water in her bedroom, Doug was aware of the situation, and was obviously tormented by it. One day the actress May McAvoy and Mrs Harold Lloyd dropped in to see Mary at Pickfair while Doug was out playing golf. When Mary offered her guests a drink, the butler said he had had strict instructions from Mr Fairbanks that no drinks were to be served to his wife.

In the early 1930s Doug started to travel without his wife for the first time in their marriage. As an excuse for his gallivanting, he made two rather feeble pictures, *Around The World In Eighty*

189

Minutes (1931) and *Mr Robinson Crusoe* (1932), the latter allowing him a long stay in the South Seas. Mary, commenting on his travels, said, 'Douglas had always faced a situation the only way he knew how, by running away from it.... I always prefer to look an issue squarely in the face.' What Mary had to face squarely was that Doug had been seen around fashionable spots in Europe with the attractive blonde twenty-nine-year-old wife of Lord Ashley, the former chorus girl Sylvia Hawkes. For over twelve years Doug and Mary had been faithful to each other, something of a rarity in Hollywood. Now gossip columnists were hinting at a liaison with Lady Ashley. In 1932 when Doug decided on another trip to Europe, Mary took the Santa Fe Chief to New York to seek legal advice. During a stop in Albuquerque, there was a knock at the door of her train compartment. It was Doug, who had been flown in a friend's private plane to catch her up. He continued the journey with her, vowing his eternal love and denying any interest in Sylvia. Nevertheless, he sailed for England, ostensibly for a golf tournament, after asking Mary to wait for him. Back in Hollywood, Mary naively confided her fears of losing her husband to her old friend, gossip columnist Louella Parsons, imploring her to keep the news to herself. Louella kept quiet for six weeks, until she got wind that a rival newspaper was about to run an article on the Fairbanks' marital problems. Mary then issued a statement that she and Doug loved each other as much as ever.

Mary's final film, *Secrets* (1933), was a creaky saga which cast her as a courageous woman faithful to one man through three generations, despite her husband's affairs with other women. It was a role Mary plainly wished the public to identify with her real-life problems. But whatever the circumstances dividing the couple, their love for each other kept pulling them back together, and they still entertained at Pickfair when Doug wasn't off on one of his jaunts to far-away places. However, in January 1934 Mary got a call from Doug in London, where he was making his last film, *The Private Life Of Don Juan*, to tell her he had been named as co-respondent in Lord Ashley's divorce suit. It was then that Mary decided to get a divorce. Ironically, Doug turned to his first wife to persuade Mary not to do it. He sent a two-hundred-word telegram begging Beth, now married for the third time, to intercede on his behalf with Mary. Beth did her best to persuade Mary to take Doug back but she had been publicly humiliated, as

Beth had once been and refused. 'Can you imagine?' Mary asked Beth innocently. 'My husband running off with another woman!' Beth did not reply.

Mary was in tears as she left the courtroom after the divorce hearing on 10 January 1935. When Doug, who was in St Moritz with Sylvia, was informed of the divorce, he shut himself up in his hotel room, disconnected the telephone, and refused to speak to reporters. Some months later he returned to America and literally begged Mary on his knees not to take up the final divorce papers. 'I've never loved anyone but Mary and I never will,' he told his brother, but Mary could not bring herself to resume the marriage, although she still loved him.

Doug persisted even after the divorce became final in January 1936. He suggested they run away together, or build a ranch in California now that their acting careers were over. Again she rejected his pleas and he fled despondently to New York after telling her that, if she changed her mind, all she need say was, 'Come home for Christmas dinner.' On the journey east, which Doug made with his son, he continued his tireless re-courtship of Mary by sending her lengthy telegrams from every stop. The telegrams remained unanswered. Finally, Doug gave up the struggle, called Sylvia in England, and asked her to marry him. She accepted, and he left for Europe the following day. After he had sailed, Douglas Jr went to the Waldorf–Astoria to collect his father's mail and discovered that a telegram from Mary had been put in the wrong pigeon-hole. It read, 'Come home for Christmas dinner.' When she discovered that Doug was already at sea, Mary telephoned him on shipboard to repeat the message. 'It's too late,' Doug mournfully told her. 'It's just too late.'

Douglas Fairbanks married Sylvia Ashley in March 1936, and the couple settled at the Fairbanks' Santa Monica beach house, not too far from Mary at Pickfair. Shortly after Doug brought his new wife – whom he would always introduce as Lady Ashley – back to California, they were invited to a cocktail party by Gloria Swanson. Gloria had mischievously omitted to tell them that Mary had been invited too. There was mutual astonishment when they found themselves facing each other. The two women exchanged pleasantries and discussed the possible sale of Pickfair while an extremely agitated Doug stood by.

It soon became apparent that the strong bond between Pickford and Fairbanks would not easily be severed. Although neither would ever return to the screen after the failure of their last films, they were both still actively involved in United Artists, the company they helped found. Once, at a board meeting, when a U.A. partner disagreed violently with Mary on some issue, Doug shouted, 'How dare you talk to my wife like that?' and threw the man out of the room. Sometimes Doug would go to Pickfair and sit quietly with Mary beside the swimming pool for hours. 'What a mistake, Mary!' he said one day. She replied, 'Yes, I'm sorry.'

Doug and Mary each made efforts to salvage their lives without one another. Mary produced a couple of films, wrote a novel and a spiritual self-help manual. Doug continued to keep his body in trim by doing strenuous daily exercies, but he ate rich food, smoked excessively and, due to a busy social life, slept little. With no work to do, be became bored and longed for the days of acting and public acclaim. 'There's nothing as humiliating as a has-been,' he told a friend. Doug suffered a blow when Mary married Charles 'Buddy' Rogers in June 1937. 'The attentions of such an attractive young man were naturally a wonderful help during those years of loneliness that followed the final break with Douglas,' Mary recalled. 'He gave me back my desire to live.' Doug could never accept that Mary was in love with Buddy. 'She's only pretending, to make me jealous,' he told his brother.

On 10 December 1939 Doug suffered a severe pain in his chest which he thought was indigestion. A doctor was called and diagnosed a coronary thrombosis. Doug was immediately confined to bed. One of the several people who visited him during the day was Douglas Jr who read to him. Sylvia went to a Red Cross meeting that evening, leaving a male nurse outside the bedroom. Shortly after midnight Douglas Fairbanks died at the age of fifty-six. He left a last message for Mary: 'If anything happens to me, tell Mary, "By the clock."' She was in Chicago when her niece telephoned from Hollywood. Before Gwynne could break the news Mary said, 'Don't tell me. My darling has gone.' 'Yes, Auntie, Douglas is dead.' Buddy Rogers, who was in the room, left his wife alone to weep. And weep she did, mourning the passing of one of the world's most powerful and poignant love affairs.